"Marriage is difficult, ɪ
statistics. But through the challenges, there can be great
blessings! Allow this book to show you how to strengthen
your marriage and give you principles for discovering
the joy of the gift of marriage."

—**Gregg Matte,**
Pastor of Houston's First Baptist Church,
Author of *Unstoppable Gospel*

"Aaron Bunker's *A Stronger Knot* is an honestly-written,
practical guide to make your marriage all God intended
it to be. If you are considering marriage, this book will
give you the wisdom to build your marriage on a strong
foundation. If you want to make your marriage better,
this book will give you the tools to do so. If you think
your marriage is beyond hope of ever being happy or
healthy again, this book will plant the seed in your heart
that God can heal and restore your relationship. This is
a 'must-read' for anyone who wants their marriage to
flourish."

—**Paul Osteen,** MD

"Aaron Bunker draws on his personal experience to help couples navigate the path to a healthy marriage. Using rules he and his wife established for their marriage, Aaron gives a candid account of how their marriage has progressed and then offers those rules to the reader as an example of what they can create to help make their marriage successful. This book is valuable for couples not satisfied with the status quo."

—Dr. Milton S. Magness,
DMin, MA Psy, MA(RE), LPC, CSAT,
Hope and Freedom Counseling Services

"It has been a while since I've read a book that I can recommend to couples without hesitation or a disclaimer of any type, but this is one of those. Aaron gives practical, biblically-based truths in a way that is both convicting and encouraging. With a mixture of vulnerability and humor, he makes the reader feel hopeful about their marriage and encouraged to seek a closer relationship. Whether couples are struggling or doing fairly well, I highly recommend *A Stronger Knot* and believe that your marriage can grow from the teaching you'll find inside."

—Dr. Jessica McCleese,
Licensed Psychologist, Founder of Fully Well

"In *A Stronger Knot*, Aaron Bunker has taken his passion for marriage—his own and others'—and provided a practical primer on the primacy of marriage. The truths he establishes are equally relevant whether you are in the process of making a marriage or in the marathon of marriage. Thank you, Aaron, for sharing this with us!"

—Adam Mason,
MAMFC, LPC-S, Minister of Counseling Services at
Houston's First Baptist Church

"Through vulnerability and deep personal stories, Aaron Bunker gives readers practical advice and easy-to-apply steps when it comes to the big topic of marriage. I recommend this book for any couple starting out on their marriage journey."

—Mike Berry,
Co-creator of the award-winning blog,
Confessions of an Adoptive Parent

"In *A Stronger Knot*, Aaron beautifully shows us that love is vulnerability. He graciously points us to our Father and encourages us to live in intentionality. He challenges us that marriage is a daily decision to serve one another. The choice is ours."

—Cynthia Barkley,
PhD, LPC-S

A STRONGER KNOT

TYING TOGETHER A UNITED MARRIAGE

AARON BUNKER

LUCIDBOOKS

ISBN-10: 1-63296-177-6
ISBN-13: 978-1-63296-177-8
eISBN-10: 1-63296-178-4
eISBN-13: 978-1-63296-178-5

To my wife Hannah, who believes in me even when I have trouble seeing it. This book does not come to fruition without your faithful love.

To couples: May you find Jesus and love throughout this book as you grow in your relationships!

Table of Contents

Foreword

As a therapist and advocate for intimate, fulfilling marriages, I greatly appreciate the theme and emphasis in *Tying a Stronger Knot*. Married clients will often make statements to me like, "I think we married for some of the wrong reasons," or, "We seem incompatible." I wonder if they want me to throw up my hands in alarm and instantly agree. I simply tell them, "Join the club!" We all marry for some of the wrong reasons and many of our right reasons won't last 50 years. And, of course you are incompatible—you married someone of the opposite sex, you were attracted to someone with a different personality, you come from unique family backgrounds, and you are selfishly human.

The fulfilling and lasting marriages are those that accept the incompatibilities and actually allow them to add a richness to the relationship. The great marriages that survive and flourish are the ones that have made the intentional choices to create a stronger knot. They keep creating new reasons to love and support each other as

Jesus and the Holy Spirit help them forgive the hurts and grow something strong and beautiful.

Don't we all yearn for a loving, beautiful marriage? This brings us to another goal of Aaron's in writing this book—not only to create a stronger knot but to help you understand what that "knot" can represent. You can build a marriage that actually reflects what God originally intended for marriage to be in the Garden of Eden. This can be a fun quest. "Lord, make my marriage like Adam and Eve in Eden." Originally, there was no selfish, undependable brokenness. Adam and Eve were totally honest and trustworthy. They hadn't learned all the toxic ways to lie by blaming, rationalizing, and betraying. They had a beautiful, child-like innocence with no need to have each other's back because there was nothing to defend against. A perfect trust created a peace and freedom to be transparent and intimate.

They walked and talked in the Garden and enjoyed an intimate communication that was totally honest and easily included their Creator. No shame, insecurity, or need to hide anything existed at that time. This type of communication is what we therapists call "Active Listening," an ability to share openly and empathize easily.

Yes! Total openness and a playful lack of inhibition reigned. You've seen little children dancing around naked with joy and excitement. They have a child-like innocence with a natural curiosity and awe-filled anticipation of life that we lose as adults. Adam and Eve had this in their relationship and marriage. They celebrated passionate feelings we struggle to imitate. They were free and authentic—whole, real, with an ability to share life playfully and completely. In Eden, they were truly "naked and unashamed!" You may be thinking that in this fallen world, we can never duplicate Eden. But precious friend, that is why Jesus came to earth. He came to redeem and restore. He came to give us the Holy Spirit, to empower us to be new and whole again. Yes, it is possible to be trustworthy, transparent, uninhibited, and unselfish. All marriages can build something new and better.

Dear reader, as you read this book, use its wisdom and encouragement to tie that knot even stronger. Let God take your marriage back to Eden as you become truly "naked and unashamed," physically and especially emotionally. God has given you a special gift in each other and your marriage. Keep building that sacred commitment as you laugh and play and allow your loving Creator to grow you into His original intention for marriage.

Doug Rosenau

Introduction

"As high as God is above man, so high are the sanctity, the rights, and the promise of marriage above the sanctity, the rights, and the promise of love. It is not your love that sustains the marriage, but from now on, the marriage that sustains your love."

—Dietrich Bonhoeffer

Sunday, September 25, 2016, was the last day of a couples retreat and mission trip that my wife, Hannah, and I attended in New York City with our small Bible study group from our church. We were sitting in Central Park having a cup of coffee—I will walk just about anywhere for a good cup of coffee—and enjoying the beautiful fall weather since we don't have what others call "seasons" in Houston, where we lived. Houston is just hot and hotter. I was enjoying all of God's beauty in nature, and thinking about how many great ideas and ventures had been birthed out of Central Park, when it hit me: this was the time. It was time to write my book.

I have dreamed of writing a book ever since I started dating my wife, back in 2007. I felt the Lord tell me then that he wanted to use my voice to help change marriages because marriages are under attack. The sanctity of marriage is under siege as the enemy seeks to destroy it. Marriage is one of the most sacred things one does in life and is one of the unions God has designed to help meet our needs. When spouses mutually strive to meet each other's needs, they become more Christlike because they lay down their own life for each other. The three institutions God designed to help meet our needs are Marriage (Gen. 1), Family (Gen. 3), and the Church (Matt. 16). Marriage was God's design before sin entered into the world in Genesis 3.

Our purpose in marriage is the same purpose we have in our singleness—to be more Christlike. We should get married because we believe we can do more to advance the Kingdom of God together than we can separately. Marriage is more than happy feelings and joyous moments. Marriage is a daily decision to serve one another (1 Cor. 7:4 MSG). Marriages are filled with broken people who should strive to be the best person they can be and in turn, the best spouse they can be. People get married for many different reasons: love, pregnancy, belief that God is calling them to marriage, the pleasure of a vacation partner and best friend, or the good feeling they have when they're around that special person.

The reason we get married is often forgotten when trials and tribulations come. Sometimes we realize that those reasons were not enough to keep the marriage going. Just feeling good around someone or being good friends does not keep a marriage strong and alive when troubles come. When we're faced with trials and tribulations, we find out what our marriage is really founded upon. If it was built on things that fade over time, we may think our marriage is fading too. If it was built on things we've long forgotten, we may feel no hope that it will ever get better. We might even end the marriage to avoid future pain.

Even if you have built your marriage on things that have since slipped away or are no longer visible, that doesn't mean your marriage has to be over. There is still hope; you just have to rebuild it. The very same power that raised Christ from the dead lives inside each person who has made the choice to follow Jesus, and that same power can resurrect a dead marriage and breathe life into one that is gasping for breath.

I want to encourage you to persevere. I have to choose to fight every day for my marriage and my family. I have to push back insecurities and pains and hurts. Sometimes your insecurities may be something you have believed your entire life, and they are thoughts that have consumed you. What if those insecurities and negative things you have heard are not true? What if, as in John 15, they are the vines that need to be pruned to help you produce better fruit? The enemy knows where to hit us. What if the lies and fears are keeping you from fulfilling what God has called you to be? The power and love of God is more than you could ever imagine and can more than compensate for any fears or insecurities you may have about your marriage. I want to challenge you to keep fighting. *"We must not get tired of doing good"* (Gal. 6:9).

As you read this book, I don't want you to hear my words. I want you to hear the voice and the heart of the Father who loves you deeply and wants more for your marriage and more for your walk in the freedom that is found in loving Jesus.

CHAPTER 1

Beginning

"Mawage. Mawage is wot bwings us togeder tooday."[1]

—*The Princess Bride*

Maybe you picked this book up to read because of the way it looked on the shelf. Maybe you liked the title. Maybe somebody bought it for you, and you didn't want to be rude, so you decided to read it out of kindness or obligation. Whatever the reason, I am going to make a huge assumption right off the bat: you want more for your life and more for your marriage. Maybe your marriage is in a tough place, and this book is your last ditch effort to keep it afloat. Maybe you are doing well in marriage and just want to keep growing.

But I am going out on a limb and stating that, at the very least, you want more. I think most of us want more.

I love marriage! I really do. My passion is to see marriages continue to look more like Jesus on a daily basis. I started dating my wife, Hannah, while we were still in a community college in Houston. She was a theater major, and I was a voice major. I planned to be a worship pastor. I'd felt the Lord calling me to ministry and assumed since I could carry a decent tune that I was going to be a vocational worship pastor.

I met Hannah in a theater class called "Voice and Diction." It was required for theater majors and strongly recommended for voice majors, but I ended up being the only voice major to take the class. What a great choice it was for me! I've forgotten much of what I learned in that class, but I will never forget that gorgeous redhead. Our first assignment was to read something out loud so the professor could record our diction and pace of speech. Hannah read from The Bible, y'all. She read 1 Corinthians 13, the Bible's chapter on love. I knew then that there was something different and special about her. We began dating the next semester, after we performed in *The Wizard of Oz* together. I fell in love with the beautiful redhead playing Dorothy rather quickly. I remember dropping her off at her house after one of our dates and saying out loud to myself, "I am going to marry that girl one day."

I have known two things in my life to be true and I cannot remember a time that they did not exist.

First, I am going bald and may be a complete cue ball by the time you read this. I never dreamed of having hair like Jesse from *Full House* or any of the guys on *Grease*. I knew I'd better have a great personality and be likable because my dome was not going to win anybody's attention.

Second, I have known since birth that I like girls.

But I had this tough dilemma: I liked girls, but they didn't like me, so I got hurt a lot. It hurt to feel this way toward others and never to have my feelings reciprocated. After a particular girl in high school, I resolved to never be burned like that again. Before my first date with Hannah, I felt God asking me to do one of the toughest things I had ever heard him say; "Aaron, you have to be willing to be hurt again." At that moment, the revelation came to me: relationships do not move forward without being vulnerable.

So I put my heart completely on the line before I even formally asked her to be my girlfriend. I was vulnerable and shared with her the darkest moments in my life, as if to say, "Here I am. Take it or leave it." This is not for everybody. It is what *I* needed to do because it helped me put my heart on the table to let God hold it rather than any person. I told Hannah that I also felt God calling me to Colorado Springs to pursue being a worship pastor. I told her because I didn't want to just date her for a couple of months and then end it. I wanted to date her only if there were a possibility this could lead to marriage. I am serious; I laid it all out there, my heart on the chopping block. She so sweetly said yes and then in her quirky humor asked, "Can I update my Myspace status now?"

When I asked Hannah out on a date, I didn't have a clue what I was doing. I was a dating novice. We dated for two months before I moved to Colorado Springs, about 1,000 miles from Houston, for a 10-month program in a megachurch that was designed to train and equip worship pastors for vocational ministry. I knew that our long-distance relationship would either bring us closer together or tear us apart. I did not really see any other possibility. I wanted to marry this girl! I had to learn how to date someone, how to get to know both her and myself while still pursuing God, and do this all long distance. I strived to be the best boyfriend I could possibly imagine.

I love to sing, I love music, and I love God. It seemed like the perfect fit to be a worship leader, which is why I packed my Chrysler Sebring and traveled across the country with my mother and my new girlfriend on one of the scariest drives of my life, pulling behind me a U-Haul trailer through the mountains of Colorado.

The problem with my dream of being a worship leader had been apparent ever since I was young. Although I can carry a decent tune, my timing is horrible! On a side note, that is why to this day I have difficulty dancing, because I want to just dance to the music in my heart, join in, and have fun. This may or may not have caused some tension at times with my wife, since she loves to dance her booty off and I have difficulty leading her on the dance floor. I'm not sure why I thought that being a worship pastor would be any different for this rhythmically challenged guy. I learned rather quickly that being a worship pastor was not going to be my profession. However, I knew God had me there for a reason. I lived life on my own, and for the first time, completely felt what it was like to be held accountable for finances and personal responsibility. Most of all, I learned how to be intentional in a relationship with someone because I was nowhere close to her for our first year as a couple. I had to learn how to be the man she deserved and the man God was calling me to be from 1,000 miles away.

I ordered every book on relationships that you could imagine. At this point, I hadn't told Hannah that I loved her. We'd only been dating two months. I read books on love, dating, marriage, and friendship. Truths jumped off the pages, teaching me about marriage and what makes marriage and relationships work. Looking back, I can tell you this: I felt God calling me to help change marriages and pour into marriages with everything I had. The joke Hannah always says is that I was always called to be an advocate for marriages and pour into them; I just needed her in my life to realize it. I knew I wanted to be a marriage counselor and speak to couples before we were even engaged.

I finished up my school in Colorado Springs, came back to Houston, proposed to Hannah, and got married in July 2008, the hotter of the two seasons in Houston. Then we began our life together as a couple, loving God and doing our best to pour into each other. What started as a show business relationship had reached the altar; now it was time to live it out.

We finished our undergraduate schooling during that first year of marriage while I worked at the coffee empire of the world, Starbucks. I received a bachelor's degree in psychology, which, I found out, is worthless without an advanced degree. So shortly after, I continued my education, earning my master's degree in marriage and family therapy. I've learned a lot about marriage from the books I've read, from experiencing my own marriage, and from my years as a marriage counselor.

Hannah and I work well together, but we are not a "normal couple." I mean, I'm a guy counselor in a field dominated by women. I'm the cook in the house, and my wife, who hates cooking, just got back from Lowe's and is painting the wall next to me. She also just fixed the garbage disposal, replaced the flush valve on the toilet, and landscaped our backyard in the last week. My wife is incredibly handy. We are opposites of the stereotypical couple you read about in relationship books.

She was also born to write, create, and then change it all up again because she gets bored with the status quo. There have been too many times to count when I came home from work and the furniture was rearranged, a room was painted a different color, or some new doohickey appeared in our house. Excuse me, our "home." She has been telling me since we moved in that she is "making our house a home." Apparently it required a lot of work to become a home because she has been saying that for nearly seven years and it's still not there yet. I have a feeling it may never get the final pat on the back that tells the house, "Congrats! You did it! You have fulfilled your dream of becoming a home."

I am emotional and cry and have these weird and interesting things called "feelings." I know, right! "There's no crying in baseball."[2] Well, there is crying for this dude, and emotions are worn and shown and experienced in their full glory. I almost teared up thinking of the house not fulfilling its dream of becoming a home. But my wife is not the default emoter, and it takes effort for her to communicate her feelings.

We are not your typical husband and wife. If you are one of the stereotypical couples, then awesome. Even if you are not, it does not mean that you are weird or that there is something wrong with you. God has designed each person uniquely in his image. You are special. Don't try to be someone else's version of yourself. Be you and all that God has given you. No other couple on the planet has your story, so don't feel that you have to conform to some ideal. Just make sure you are loving God and loving your spouse. The examples included in this book may sound just like you. Or you may be the couple that states, "We are nothing like those crazy Bunkers." Either is okay.

Not Perfect

What makes my relationship with Hannah work is not that we are following some pattern for successful personality typology, but that we want to see each other become all that God has created the other person to be. We want to empower one another to live in the freedom of being an heir of King Jesus. We don't want to squash our differences to make our spouses be more like us. In fact, we want to pour into the areas that we are different as we nurture and cultivate those parts to be used for the Kingdom of God. I can't control Hannah, and she can't control me. This may sound simple, except for the fact that control is exactly what we all seem to want over our spouses. I proposed at an off Broadway Show called *I Love You, You're Perfect, Now Change.* This show is a hilarious way of describing what a lot of people do when they get married. They say they love everything about one another, and then they get married and find that some of those things aren't so cute anymore: "How can you not like the fact that I want to have the dishes cleaned immediately after we eat and that time with you, the kids, and our company can wait? The dishes are a priority!" That was probably too close to home for you, but not me. Definitely not me.

Just kidding. That's me. Dishes are a thing with me.

We are not perfect by any means. We struggle all the time but try to show grace to one another through the process. We have made many mistakes in our marriage, and not a day goes by that we do it perfectly. We argue. We disagree. We have petty disagreements that go in directions we never intended so that we don't even remember what we're fighting about or why it started. We struggle with pride and arrogance and throwing adult temper tantrums. This book is not about how to be the perfect couple, because that couple does not exist. No matter where your marriage is though, there is hope. There is light at the end of the tunnel. Even though you may feel hopeless, there is hope in Jesus for your marriage. God hates divorce (Mal. 2:16) and he wants your marriage to turn around and be fun and joyful, with no fear or shame. We are all broken people in need of Jesus Christ in our lives and in our marriages. I'm not here to condemn you for your mistakes or to tell you that you have to have a marriage like mine. Every marriage has its own unique value and nuances. I am here to share not only our journey and some of the many lessons that we have learned through our marriage, but also my experience as a marriage counselor who is on the front lines with couples, daily. I pray that these lessons will also benefit your relationship.

Creating Our Family Rules

Hannah loves to create! I could write a whole book on her creative genius, but I'll save that for another day. She's called to create, but she says everybody is because we are made in God's image. God is the ultimate Creator, so we all have a little creativity in our DNA makeup. This has been a struggle for me because I have never been good at creating. That was Hannah's identity, not mine. Be careful for those moments in your life when you have given yourself a negative identity, telling yourself that you can't do something or that you aren't supposed to. Let God be the authority on what you should and shouldn't do because there are a lot of purposes that he wants you to accomplish.

> "Be careful for those moments in your life when you have given yourself a negative identity, telling yourself that you can't do something or that you aren't supposed to. Let God be the authority on what you should and shouldn't do because there are a lot of purposes that he wants you to accomplish."

Do you know where you want your marriage and family to go? What are you striving toward? We want to have something we can run toward as opposed to having something to run away from. Habakkuk 2 tells us to write down a vision in order to run after it. For several years, we tried to live the best marriage we could but didn't have a blueprint for what we wanted that to look like. We were striving for something more for our marriage, and we wanted to have something that we could agree on as the foundations and principles for our marriage and family.

Then we saw a sign in a friend's house that listed their family rules. These were rules that they tried to live by and apply to their lives. Hannah and I both loved it and decided to make our own. There are many examples of these on Pinterest, and I figured we would find one that we liked and purchase it. But instead of buying it, like most people do, Hannah built one herself—and it looks amazing! I think she chose to do this for several reasons. The first reason is that she loves to create and doesn't want to stop. The other reason is that those rules on Pinterest are other families' rules, and we wanted our own specific rules for our family. We wanted rules that applied to our dynamic, but we've since learned that our rules can be everybody's rules as well. I've posted a photo of her artwork at the end of the book. We prayed and thought about what we wanted to put in our family rules, and here is what we came up with:

In Our Family . . .
We Live for God
We Love People
We Speak Life
We Laugh Loudly
We Are Honest
We Are Thankful
We Forgive
We Have Purpose
We Are Real

These rules are posted in the living room of our home and are a daily reminder of what we strive for. This is also a banner for any who enter into our home to know that we are serious about God and about our family! We've had many conversations stem from these rules, and they will forever be a part of our family's DNA.

These rules are so near and dear to our hearts that I'm going to spend the remainder of this book encouraging you and challenging you through them. I encourage you to read them and try to apply them to your life and family, and then to pray about any additional rules for your family.

We do not always do these rules perfectly—and honestly we never will—but we have laid the foundation and are striving to build our lives around them. Who knows? Maybe you'll be inspired to go to your local Lowe's or Home Depot to create your own rules to hang on display. If you're going to hang a giant sign in your home, be prepared to have conversations around it. You won't regret it. In fact, you may be helping other families. I believe that once we receive encouragement, we are not supposed to hang on to it just for ourselves. We are supposed to empower others. My prayer is that your family and marriage begin to look more like Christ. Now, if you will turn your phones to silent and lean back in your chairs, we will begin to look at the first rule.

CHAPTER 2

In Our Home We Live for God

*If you decide that it's a bad thing to worship
God, then choose a god you'd rather serve—
and do it today. Choose one of the gods your
ancestors worshiped from the country beyond
The River, or one of the gods of the Amorites, on
whose land you're now living. As for me and my
family, we'll worship God.*

— Joshua 24:15, MSG

W e love God above all else, or at least that
should be our deepest desire. We've adopted
the Shema, a prayer first mentioned in
Deuteronomy:

*Listen, Israel: The Lord our God, the Lord is
One. Love the Lord your God with all your heart,*

*with all your soul, and with all your strength.
These words that I am giving you today are to
be in your heart. Repeat them to your children.
Talk about them when you sit in your house and
when you walk along the road, when you lie
down and when you get up. Bind them as a sign
on your hand and let them be a symbol on your
forehead. Write them on the doorposts of your
house and on your gates.*

Deuteronomy 6:4–9

It is Jewish tradition to read this out loud every day. Every day it is a reminder to put God first and tell your kids about how much God means to you, that he is your everything. Jesus quoted the greatest commandments in Matthew 22:34–40 from the Shema. Do we really live by this mantra every day? Now, of course we make mistakes; the Bible says we *"all have sinned and fall short of the glory of God"* (Rom. 3:23). But the question that I daily want to meditate on is this: *Am I actually attempting to put him first a majority of the time? Am I living a life that reflects that I belong to King Jesus?* There is a song called *"Ever Be"* by Bethel[1]; the idea of the song is that praise will forever be on our lips. We need to put our attention on Christ to remember that everything we do is because of God.

Faith

Living for Christ is a constant faith journey. God continually asks us to trust him more, and the only way to really do that is to trust him, even though we may not know where he is leading. I've learned that when I feel in control, I'm not always focused on trusting him. It is easier to trust God when I do not have a clue how to do it without him, when I have no other choice but to trust God because I literally have no idea how to do it on my own.

For me, this is easy, because what do I have to lose? If I don't have a clue what to do next, I don't have any other options but to trust him! For me, giant leaps of faith are the easy ones. This includes getting married, buying our first home, deciding to adopt children, and changing careers. Now, these are huge life-changing events, but what I have noticed in those moments is that I turn to God in desperation. He hears me and answers my prayers because they are prayers that are totally and completely dependent on him.

But I struggle trusting God with the small, mundane, daily areas of my life. I sometimes think I can do life on my own and forget to depend on the Lord. My prayer is that I live every day with complete abandon and total dependence on God.

When you become a follower of Jesus, the Scripture says that you become *"a new creation; old things have passed away, and look, new things have come"* (2 Cor. 5:17). My new way of thinking through Christ gives me freedom because I no longer have to do it alone. I have the great joy of giving up my burden because it is no longer my burden to carry. I get to focus my eyes and heart on God and trust him with my all. I want to have faith in the small, daily mundane areas to show that he really does have all of me always, not just when I am feeling desperate or without another option. I want faith in Jesus to be my first option, not just my extreme case scenario option.

I'm Not Hungry

I am a meat guy and could probably have a steak every day of my life. I would change up the sides because I don't want to be boring and predictable. Come on now! But steak can always stay on the menu. Hannah once went over a year without meat because of a personal conviction she felt. This was a true test of commitment. Ridiculously, when she told me about her new vegetarian endeavor, I was frustrated with her and, honestly, kind of angry. (Thank the Lord for the maturing process, since we can all be immature about our offenses.) "I didn't sign up for this. I married a meat lover!" I exclaimed.

We have a restaurant in our town that serves all you can eat meat. It is amazing. They have steak, chicken, pork, lamb, and many others. This is a meat-lover's paradise. They give you a coaster with one side red and one side green. When it's green, they keep serving you meat, so of course when we go, mine never goes on red. When I go to a restaurant like this, I plan on it the entire day, eating only a light lunch or a snack. I don't want to be so full that I can't eat my share of protein. If I am going to pay those prices, then I want to get my money's worth! One of the silliest things to do is to go to this restaurant and not be hungry.

Jesus says in Matthew 5:6, *"Those who hunger and thirst for righteousness are blessed, for they will be filled."* Jesus is saying that if we are hungry for him, we are guaranteed to be filled. The only logical conclusion to me is that we are just not hungry for more of him. We say we want more of God in our lives, but we don't go to church. We are praying for something more, but then we don't open our Bibles or spend time in worship. How can we ever expect to be filled with Christ if we never come to him hungry? How hungry are you? I pray for hunger and thirst regularly because there are plenty of times when I am hungry, but not for Christ. I may want relaxation time or fun time and may not be hungry for the right thing. I want to come hungrily to the table he has prepared for me in the presence of my enemies (Ps. 23:5). I want to starve my flesh and feed my spirit. When you feed your life with Christ and his purposes for your life, then you begin to crave it when it is not there.

My challenge to you is to ask God for a hunger and a thirst for him that is never sated. When we come to him hungry for more of him, he *will* feed us. He is the cup that never runs dry, and he is the true source of nourishment that is the bread of life (John 6:35).

There will be times when you may not want to read the Bible or praise or honor your spouse. That is normal. There will be moments when you slip up and choose unwisely, as when Donovan chose the wrong cup in *Indiana Jones and the Last Crusade.*[2] He chose the false grail and perished. But the more often you choose to sacrifice and submit your heart to the Word of God, the easier it will become to make the right choices. Whatever habit you choose to do more consistently is the one that will stick because you're creating new pathways and habits in your brain that pour out into your spirit. You can read your Bible faithfully for one week, but if you don't continually set aside time to do it, then you will go back to your old habits and stop reading. The same principle applies to anything that we want to be different in our lives. We have to be consistent and continue to choose it, or we go right back to the "normal" that we are used to.

I think we're all hungry for something. What are you hungry for? Are you hungry for the Word of God, a heart of worship, and his love in your life? Or, are you hungry for things of the world? We teach our kids what to hunger for, and they follow our examples. What they see us get excited about is what they learn to hunger after. Do you teach them to be hungry for the bread of life and streams of living water? Or do you teach them to get hungry over things that are only temporary and are fading into oblivion? If my kids see me watching and celebrating sporting events more than they see me in the Word and worshiping, then I'm teaching them to value sports and television more than God. We all lead by example. What example are you leaving for your family to follow?

Covenant vs Contract

Anybody who has been married more than five minutes knows that marriage can be difficult at times. As I mentioned previously, you cannot change your spouse. This means all we can do is change ourselves. The reason this is so difficult is that it is easy to focus on our spouses' struggles and insecurities instead of working on our own. In his book *Sacred Marriage*, Gary Thomas asks the question, "What if marriage was not meant to make us happy, but instead to make us more holy?"[3] Holiness is the driver for marriage and the purpose of marriage is to make us look more like Christ. That does not mean that you can't be happy in marriage. I pray you are. It just means that your drive and reasons for doing the things you do in marriage are not just for your happiness or the happiness of your spouse. This kind of holiness stems from the fact that marriage is a covenant relationship, not a contracted one.

Most of us have cell phone contracts. When you pay your bill, the cell phone conglomerate agrees to offer you service. If you do not pay your bill, eventually they will terminate your contract and turn your phone off. This would be a sad day because how else would you stay up until all hours of the night looking at your social media feeds or playing Candy Crush? If you pay your bill and they do not provide you service or the service is unreliable, then you will probably end your contract and look for another provider. That is how a contract works. Two parties agree upon a set of rules that each will abide by; if either party does not hold up its end of the deal, the contract will be null and void and the contract can be ended.

However, that is not how a covenant works. A covenant states that you are going to hold up your end of the deal even if your partner does not at times. This is what the language "for better or worse" means. I believe many couples don't think about what a covenant is because most partners do a pretty good job of "doing their part" well during the dating and engagement stage—and even into marriage. Most people don't think about what to do if their partner acts selfish, proud, angry, or rude. When you get married, you are called to do your part anyway. For example, Ephesians 5 states that husbands are to love their wives and that wives are to respect their husbands. What it does *not* say is *if*. It does not say, "Husbands love your wife *if* she respects you," or, "Wives respect your husband *if* he loves you." All you can do is control yourself and do everything you can to be the husband or wife that God has called you to be. You have to love God first above all else and then release your spouse to God.

God wants all of you. We are not to have any other gods above him, and that includes your spouse. Wait, what? If you are not careful, then your spouse can easily become an idol. You know that your spouse has become an idol in your life if you are trying to please him or her more than the Father in Heaven. Many times, my wife has become an idol in my life. I love her so much. I try to serve her and love her with everything I have. The problem is that if I'm not first loving and serving God, I may take it personally if she has a bad day and doesn't respond kindly to my affection. We have to be very careful to not serve one another solely for the praise of being a good spouse. We have to guard our hearts against manipulation or pride in marriage and parenting. You may be thinking, "Aaron, how can I love and serve my spouse and that be considered selfish?" Great question!

The answer to that question goes back to the reason why you are doing what you are doing in the first place. Are you doing it so your spouse will compliment you or do something in return? Or are you doing it because it is your job as a Godly man or woman? I will give an example to help this make more sense. Let's say it is Wednesday evening and I have come home from a long day. All I want to do is decompress, sit in front of the television, and binge on Netflix. However, when I get home, I decide to do the dishes because they are piling over and staring me in the face. There are a few things here: First of all, doing the dishes is part of being an adult. Because I'm a part of this home and family, I have a responsibility to contribute to its maintenance. I have to do the dishes no matter whether I am married or not. If I am living it up in my single bachelor pad, then I still have dishes to do, and nobody will be there to pat me on the back for my clean kitchen. Did I do them because I wanted a clean house, a compliment for doing a job well done, so there might be an after party when the kids go down? Or did I do it because I love God and love my wife? What is your motivation? We have to be very careful that when we "do the right thing" in a relationship, we do it because it is the right thing and not because we are hoping for something in return. God has called me to do my responsibilities, but he has not called me to fulfill my wife's responsibilities. I have responsibilities that God has called me to do, and I need to lean on him in order to fulfill them. God calls us to do our part and trust him with our partner and those around us.

> "God has called me to do my responsibilities, but he has not called me to fulfill my wife's responsibilities."

It really is a tough concept and conviction to follow if we don't get the reason behind it. You must lay down your life on a daily basis and serve your spouse regardless of what you get in return. We don't do it to get invited to the marital Olympics to show off and win a week getaway in the Bahamas (although that would be pretty cool to win a trip for being a rock star at marriage). We do it because that is what God has called us to do. He asks us to lay ourselves down and love him more than anything in the world. If we do it solely for our spouses and not him, then we will become resentful and frustrated when our spouses don't respond well—or the way we expect them to.

Remember, the purpose of marriage is to look more like Jesus on a daily basis, not for pats on the back when we think we deserve them. Jesus died for the church; he gave up all he had even though we did not do our part. Romans 5:8 says, *"But God proves his own love for us in that while we were still sinners Christ died for us!"* He laid his life down while I was stuck in my muck, focused only on myself and my selfish desires. God saved me knowing the deepest darkest sins that I would ever commit, and he did that for you too. We fulfill our responsibilities because we are ultimately serving a master of one. So we love and we love well, but we need to keep the correct order. Love God; *then* love people. The hierarchy of love is this: God, spouse, kids, everybody else.

Is It Safe?

Following Jesus involves risk and is not always the most popular decision. If you live in the United States, you know what it is like to have conversations about convenience, safety, and pleasure. We tend to avoid things that make us feel uncomfortable or unsafe, unless you're a thrill-seeker. Many of us do not want to risk getting hurt. Following Jesus and living your life for him is anything but safe.

What do you mean Jesus is not safe? Jesus actually tells us that we will have problems (John 16:33). I don't know about you, but it's not a refreshing or encouraging way to start your family rules by stating that you may get hurt and have troubles. Although this is true, it is not the best strategy for winning people, but stick with me. C. S. Lewis said it so beautifully in the first book of *The Chronicles of Narnia* series: *The Lion, the Witch, and the Wardrobe*, which is in some ways an allegory for Christ's crucifixion. Aslan the lion represents Christ, and before Susan meets him for the first time, she is afraid. Mr. Beaver tells her,

> *"Aslan is a lion — the Lion, the great Lion."*
>
> *"Ooh" said Susan. "I'd thought he was a man. Is he quite safe? I shall feel rather nervous about meeting a lion. . . ."*
>
> *"Safe?" said Mr Beaver. . . . "Who said anything about safe? 'Course he isn't safe. But he's good. He's the King, I tell you."*[4]

Jesus is not safe, but he is good. That is something that you never have to doubt. Jesus wants us to trust him more than we trust our own devices or our own safety. He wants us to lean on him when we are scared, and even when we are not, because he is in control and will never fail us.

There are times when I have been in the way of my wife getting to God. I know there are times when I have had my own agenda and, in the process, prevented her from her relationship with the Lord. Not only do I want God to be the priority in my life, I want him to be priority in the lives of my wife and my kids. That means I can't be their number one. I can't take her away from the Lord. I know this and wish that I practiced it more frequently. Unfortunately, if I am honest, there are too many times that I am lonely or want to spend time with her for my sake and don't really think about her relationship with the Lord. She may be in the middle of a worship session or need me to watch the kids so she can get away to spend time with the Lord. It is easy for me to want to focus on the Lord when I want to and make sure that I am spending time with him. But at times, I want my wife to spend her time with the Lord when it is convenient to me. Ouch. We need to make sure that we're not taking our spouses away from the Lord in order to get our own needs met. My wife's loving on Jesus is more important than my not wanting to miss a snuggle moment. I love me some snuggles, but her snuggles with Jesus are more important. Her need for alone time to realign with her Father is of the utmost importance, and I need to guard it carefully.

Don't be a hindrance to your spouse getting time alone with the Father. I think at times we have to check our hearts for why we want our spouses' time and affection because we may be trying to get something from them that they were never meant to fulfill in the first place. We have to be careful of not squashing anything the Lord is doing in their lives. We have to be sensitive to the move of the Holy Spirit in our spouses and not try to be the Holy Spirit for them. We have to trust the movement of God in their lives and know that he can lead them better than we ever could.

> "I think at times we have to check our hearts for why we want our spouses' time and affection because we may be trying to get something from them that they were never meant to fulfill in the first place."

Knock Your Spouse off the Throne

> *"When I have learnt to love God better than my earthly dearest, I shall love my earthly dearest better than I do now."*
>
> – C. S. Lewis

When Jesus was asked, "Teacher, which command in the law is the greatest?" he replied that it was very simple. First, he commanded us to love God with all our hearts, with all our souls, with all our strength, and all of our minds. Then he said to love our neighbors as ourselves (Matt. 22:36-40). So we love God and *then* we love people. We have to make sure that we keep the right order. If we mix up the order, which happens easily if we're not careful, then we have made our spouses idols.

There will be times when I'm doing my job by loving God and Hannah, and it won't go well. We live in a world with sin, and my wife, as amazing as she is, is a sinner. I know, it is shocking! As much as I gush over her, the lady sins on the regular. We all do. We are saints according to Ephesians 1, which I am so thankful for, yet we still sin every day. God says that he is continually working out our salvation (Phil. 2:12–13). Aren't you glad we aren't there yet? Praise God! This means that we will mess up and respond inappropriately at times. If I am doing everything in my life to please my wife, then she has become an idol. I have noticed in my life that she has snuck up there when I disappoint her or when she is upset at me. It is important to note that *you* put them up as idols; they don't get there on their own. You are the only one who can put them on the throne. If I am questioning my whole identity when my wife is upset, there is a *huge* problem. You do not get your identity from your spouse. You get your identity from Christ and Christ alone (more on identity in the chapter *In Our Home We Have Purpose*).

There are many things that can take on the role of Christ in your life. Maybe it's your spouse, your kids, or even your career. Hannah and I had difficulty becoming parents, and one day I realized that my future kids had become idols. And this was before I was a parent! I didn't realize that kids were more important to me than God until our home was empty.

There are times when not having something can also become an idol in your life. The lack of money to pay bills or support the family can become so consuming that it has your heart. My friend Jerrell calls worship "something that has our hearts' affection and our minds' attention." It's easy to put my heart toward other things or other people and to fixate my mind on something other than God. It's a constant reminder to start my day with the Lord because if I don't, my mind may begin to wander and meditate on things other than my first love.

> "It's a constant reminder to start my day with the Lord because if I don't, my mind may begin to wander and meditate on things other than my first love."

I realized early on in my counseling career that I did not want to have a counseling session if the Holy Spirit was not going to be with me in the session. I would rather not do the session than to do it without inviting him in on it. I want to live my life by the same resolution. I don't want to start my day or activities without inviting the Holy Spirit with me wherever I go. I want to represent him well, and the best way for me to do that is to invite him early and often to invade the moment and the space. I have to make sure that every morning and every night, God's praises are on my lips. I don't want to be like the church in Ephesus mentioned in Revelation 2:1–7 that forgot their first love. When you look at this story, it seems that they did everything so well. They worked hard, they endured, and they didn't tolerate evil. They were good people! But they forgot and abandoned their first love. They forgot the most important thing there is: Love God with everything you have. I want to fall more and more in love with God every day, and the only way I can do that is if I stay in constant communion and conversation with him.

Exodus states that Moses talked to God as if he were talking to a friend. I take that literally and want to talk with God as I do with my best friends. When this first became evident to Hannah and me, we reminded ourselves by starting our prayers, "What's up, God? It's Aaron and Hannah." We weren't being flippant; we were being familiar with God because he is our friend and the lover of our souls. We want to love him above everybody and everything on the planet. The best thing you can do for your marriage is spend time with Jesus on a regular basis. So, love God with all you've got and then, if you love God, make sure you are loving people. You can't love God without loving people because God is love (1 John 4:8). So if you love God well, then you should love his children well too.

CHAPTER 3

In Our Home We Love People

"Darkness cannot drive out darkness: only light can do that. Hate cannot drive out hate: only love can do that."

—Martin Luther King Jr.

I am an extrovert. I love people and I love crowds. Being in groups of people gives me energy and life. This is one of the reasons I enjoy counseling couples: my extroversion feeds off their energy.

My wife is an introvert, but she loves people. If you've ever seen any of her videos on YouTube, you may be confused by the fact that I stated she is an introvert. She is a ham. Don't get me wrong. My best man at our wedding told us there are no two bigger hams that he knows and that we were made for one another. He is right, but my wife is still very much an introvert. Many people don't really understand the definition of these two words. They assume introverts hate people and extroverts love people. Introverts are not synonymous with misanthropes. The easiest way to explain the differences is to determine from where the individual gains energy. For example, if you went on a cruise with your family for vacation, how would you describe the feeling afterward? An extrovert would say that the cruise was awesome, loved it, and can't wait to plan the next get together. An introvert may also think that it was awesome but may want to spend time alone for awhile. An introvert may need to hibernate for a while to recharge after being around people for a certain amount of time.

It is helpful to know if your spouse is an introvert or extrovert. Due to my wife's introverted personality, she loves deep, thought-provoking, life-giving conversations; however, chitchat and surface-level conversations are exhausting for her.

When we have dinner with my family, it is loud. Maybe it's the Italian in us. We talk over one another, and, honestly, I didn't notice until I met my wife. There are many times when we go to dinner with my family that she will say very little throughout the entire meal. Not because she is angry or upset or not wanting to be there, but because it takes energy from her in order to boldly interject into an already passionate conversation. But when she has the opportunity to have deep conversations, usually one-on-one, she is all over it and will come alive like a butterfly spreading its wings.

We have to honor both of our styles in loving people. We have a sign in our house that my wife made (we have many things in our house that she has made) that says "Gather." That is our heart. We want to have a home where people feel welcomed and loved. So we have people over, but not a massive group at a time. We like to have conversations that go deep to the heart of the issue, minding what is happening in each other's lives. We try to pray, right before we have any guest over, that they will feel the love of Christ, that he will reign in our conversations, and that our conversations will be energizing and recharging so that all will leave with their cup filled.

Expectations

I heard one time, at a marriage conference, that "expectations are premeditated disappointments." I agree completely. Of course there are expectations that I would call healthy expectations. You both probably have the expectation that you will be faithful to one another. That's obvious. You may have some biblical expectations of what the Bible says about marriage or maybe even divorce. But there are many times when our expectations are not clear, yet we get frustrated when our spouses do not follow through with meeting them.

It is a good idea to state expectations but also to realize that it would be exhausting to state every expectation you have. If you feel yourself getting irritated at your spouse for something they did or didn't do, ask yourself, "Did I even tell him/her what I expected or wanted in this situation?" Sometimes the expectations were clear yet unmet; those are excellent opportunities to extend grace and love. More frequently, expectations are not expressed, and hurtful arguments ensue. It is not okay to state, "Well, they should just know this is what I want." Although your spouse loves you and hopefully knows you better than anyone, they still don't know every nuance in your brain. You are both unique.

My expectation when I come home from work is to relax by watching a short episode of mindless television. But if Hannah wants to debrief her day and talk with me about mine, then she may get very annoyed with me for just coming home and relaxing for a few moments. She has been waiting all day long to tell me about her day with the kiddos, but I get home and seem to ignore her. There is nothing wrong with wanting to relax and wind down, and of course there is nothing wrong with conversing with your spouse. In fact, recharging yourself and conversing with your spouse are both important. The problem is that we each expected something different for our evening.

This is an example of why I am a fan of over-communicating. I am a planner to the extreme. I look up recipes for Thanksgiving holidays in the summer. I plan and tell Hannah many details of my expectations. But even communicating has its flaws. Sometimes I overwhelm Hannah with my overplanned expectation, so I even plan when and how much to tell her! She often prefers to go with the flow and not always be on a schedule. These are things we've learned about each other. Therefore, however and how often you choose to communicate your expectations should be unique to your marriage—just make sure they're communicated.

Something we need to be cautious of is expecting our spouses to treat us differently than we do them. Let me explain. Many clients I've worked with, and even myself at times, want their spouses to treat them one way when they make a mistake, but when their spouses mess up, they display a very different response. We often demand perfection but expect grace.

> "We often demand perfection but expect grace."

If Hannah asks me to do something and I do not remember to do it, she gets frustrated at me for not remembering something important to her. She uses her words sparingly, but they are impactful and powerful. So, if she exerted energy into sharing something with me or asking me to do something, and I forgot, it may not go over well. I will ask for forgiveness and grace. I may even express that I just had a lot going on, and it completely slipped my mind. I'll probably expect her to extend the grace toward me and move on.

However, if I've asked Hannah to do something and it doesn't get done, I have to be very careful to extend the grace to her. I can't expect her to be perfect if I am not perfect. It is easier to show others what they're doing wrong than to swallow your pride and love them through the disappointment of unmet expectations. I have to choose to love her well and be an example to my kids of grace and love. I want to love her well when she is doing it well *and* when she is not. Love and grace should never be conditional.

> "Love and grace should never be conditional."

Grace and truth go together. When I discover the truth of an unmet expectation, then I get to choose grace. I cannot extend grace without knowing truth. I have to choose to treat her better. I am not comparing myself to others' standards or morals. I am not trying to be the *best* sinner. When I am truly walking in the Spirit, I don't judge people. Matthew 5:48 states, *"Be perfect, therefore, as your heavenly Father is perfect."* I am nowhere near perfection. It's as if I am playing baseball and have a batting average of .002 (which is 2 hits out of 1,000 at-bats) and I am judging someone who has a .001 batting average (1 hit out of 1,000 at-bats). That is ridiculous! We are both so far from perfection! I get to extend grace because God extends grace to me despite my .002 batting average.

By Their Love

In John 13:34–35, Jesus states, *"I give you a new command: Love one another. Just as I have loved you, you must also love one another. By this all people will know that you are My disciples, if you have love for one another."* As Christians, there should be a difference in the way we love people. Loving God is the catalyst that ignites the love we have for others. We love people regardless of their race, economic status, or any other quantifier that makes us look or feel different. *"We love because He first loved us"* (1 John 4:19). Early Christ followers were given the name Christian by non-followers of Jesus, which translated means "little Christ." Others saw how these disciples and followers of Jesus lived their lives through love and gave them the recognition of being "little Christ." They were known by their love. Would others look at our lives and know that we loved God just based on the way that we love others? Let's strive for being known by the way we love!

Confession

At the beginning of the week, my wife and I pray over my client load. We have not always done that. We used to pray for God to provide the clients, but then relied on us to bring them in and keep them in. A couple of years ago, the Lord convicted me of this. We now pray for the numbers to stay the same or increase.

It is easy to pray for my schedule and to believe in the Lord to take care of my finances because it is related to my livelihood and well-being. In order to completely trust God with the schedule and client load, I needed to start praying for my clients to get better and to see victory in their situations. It is such a joy and an honor to see clients overcome trials and struggles to see victories.

When I began praying for my clients, even when they weren't sitting in front of me, I began to truly love them like God wanted me to. I began to trust God with my schedule, but I also began trusting him with my clients and their well-being. I've always said that I didn't want to be in the counseling session if the Holy Spirit wasn't with me; now that mantra took on a whole new meaning. When you partner with the Holy Spirit and love people well, then the Lord will keep providing people in your path to love on.

> "When you partner with the Holy Spirit and love people well, then the Lord will keep providing people in your path to love on."

The goal is to love God first and then love his people. Then you become a vessel for healing and change.

Do you trust the Holy Spirit more than you trust your intellect or skill? We need to work as if it depends on us but have faith as if it depends on God. Both are at play all the time. Do you pray for those whom you are serving and working with? Do you pour love over your city, your job, your street? You have to be careful to not speak negatively over the situation or the people in your life but instead love them where they are and show them Christ's love. Remember, do people see Christ in you by the way you show love? Or are you showing them something different entirely? Lead with love.

What They Really Want

As a self-employed counselor, I work a lot of late nights. I have to be available when couples can meet. It's hard being away from the family several nights of the week, and it's a balance that I have spent a lot of time on. Hannah and I frequently have to make sure that our priorities stay straight. I do my best to be very present the two days of the week that I do not work. I also try to take a few days off every year to love on my family, whether at a church camp, a mission trip, or staycation. I have a colleague who reminds me that finances are tight in private practice, and we sacrifice a lot of money when we don't work. I know the risks of not working, but I also know that being a present father and husband is more important to me than being successful financially. If I have to choose between having monetary possessions or being present in my wife and kids' lives, then the answer is simple: I choose family, every single time.

At the time I am writing this, my kids are three years old. They are very opinionated and have no trouble telling you what they want or need. A few days ago, I was cleaning the kitchen and preparing dinner for the evening as they were playing close by in the living room. They began declaring that they wanted to watch "Stinkadirty." *Stinky and Dirty* is the name of a kids show that comes on Amazon Prime. I started the show for them and then went back to the kitchen. A couple of minutes later, I stopped in the kitchen and lay on the couch in the living room where they were. As soon as I got there, they sat with me and wanted to play. I didn't mind playing with them. I love playing with them. But they'd just requested to watch a show and now, not five minutes later, were not interested in the show at all. There is no doubt in my mind that if I had not come over, they would have been content watching their show. The reason they no longer cared about the show is that they were getting something they wanted even more—daddy. They wanted me and all of me.

As couples and parents, we have to make sure that we are present and accounted for. We can be there physically, but are we really there mentally? It would have been easy for me to get frustrated with them and snap, telling them that I just wanted to rest and watch the show with them. If I had, I would have missed a moment to teach them how much I love them. Everyone wants to feel loved. I have asked many people who report feeling loved by their parents how their parents showed their love to them, and too many times they reply, "I just know they did because they were my parents." I don't ever want my kids to not be able to answer that question. And, when you tell them you love them, use their names.

One night, I was going through the bedtime routine with my son, and he was a little wound up, talkative, and not really listening to me. I got his attention and looked him right in the eyes and said, "Cason, I love you!"

His eyes glued on mine. "I love you too, Dad," he said with the sweetest three-year-old voice you can imagine. He then asked me to sing our goodnight song to him. I almost couldn't get through it from emotion.

Then I went into my daughter's room and attempted to recreate the same thing. "Grace, I love you!"

She looked at me kind of strange and shyly said, "Thank you?" You can't recreate moments or manufacture emotions and responses out of others; you can only worry about your own responsibilities.

The Lord convicted me that I say their names frequently when I'm frustrated with them, want them to do something, or need their attention, but I rarely say them when I'm expressing love. I want their names to be associated with love. Hannah and I chose their names very carefully and want them to know the love associated with that. Something monumental happened the night I intentionally said, "Cason, I love you." The power of saying his name with my love overwhelmed me.

> "We cannot love other people at the expense of our spouses. We cannot treat others with love and respect yet treat our spouses less."

There is power behind love, but even more power when you add a name to it.

The same goes for your spouse. You should spend time loving on your spouse on a regular basis. If the last time that you told your spouse how much you loved them was on a special occasion, then put the book down right now and go do it! We cannot love other people at the expense of our spouses. We cannot treat others with love and respect yet treat our spouses less. We love God first, then our spouse, then our kids, then everyone else. We have to make sure that we use our words very carefully and that we continue to lift our spouses up and not tear them down.

CHAPTER 4

In Our Home We Speak Life

"Kind words can be short and easy to speak, but their echoes are truly endless."

—Mother Teresa

It's easy for me to look at my wife and tell her all of the areas that she's failing. It doesn't take much effort to focus on the negative in others. This isn't because she makes more mistakes than the average human. It's because she is human, and I am the closest person to her. She allows me into her "real." When I say her "real," I mean the life that isn't always peachy. There are days that are messy and ugly, and she feels comfortable enough with me to be real about it. If I point out only her faults and struggles, then what good am I to her?

It Is Not All about That Bass

One of the first homework assignments I give to every couple who comes to see me for counseling is to make a list of 10 things that they love about their spouses. I always tell them to write the list to their spouses because they are going to read it out loud in the following session. I also give them the caveat not to include more than one physical trait or attribute. Too many clients have come back with a list of physical attributes, saying nothing about the character or personality of the spouse. It's great to recognize your spouse's physical beauty and appearance, but it can't be the only thing you see or the only thing you share with them. I ask clients to do this assignment because we need to know why we love our spouses and remind ourselves of this often.

People never schedule a session with me for couples counseling just to brag on how incredible their spouses are. They're eager to share what frustrates them and what they want to change, but when I ask them what their spouses do well, they often struggle. When we don't know what we love about our spouses, then we've focused way too much on their weaknesses and haven't fed their strengths. We need to be able to speak life into them and not death.

Life or Death—The Choice Is Yours

Your words carry a lot of power. In fact, Proverbs 18:21 states, *"Life and death are in the power of the tongue, and those who love it will eat its fruit."* Which one are you speaking when you talk to your spouse or to your kids? Are you speaking life into them and helping them live out their God-given potential, or are you extinguishing their flames by being harsh and cruel? Your words can either build up or tear down your spouse.

"But, Aaron, sometimes my spouse is mean and ugly and deserves the harsh words I'm serving over there."

I get it, your spouse is a mess and at times difficult to love or be around. I can only imagine how difficult it is to be married to such a difficult person. The easiest scripture to remember here is from Paul.

Saul, the man later called Paul, who wrote many of the books of the New Testament, was a bad dude. He murdered Christians left and right and was feared among every believer. But God got a hold of him and changed his life around in a dramatic way. It's a really cool story. You should read his story in the book of Acts if you haven't read it. After his conversion, Paul loved God with abandon and pursued a relentless love that is one to be envied. Most of the scriptures that you have memorized in the New Testament were written by Paul. An important one to remember in marriage is where Paul states that he is the worst sinner (1 Tim. 1:15). When a spouse is being difficult or hard to love, we need to remember that we too are chief sinners, and God still loves us. He poured into us and spoke life to us even when we were difficult or rude. God breathed life into the dust and created man, and he has not stopped breathing life into us to this day.

Beware of Words Spoken over You

You may have had cruel words spoken over you that you have begun to believe. Some of these may be obvious: perhaps you've been told you're an angry person, a drama queen, or not good with emotions. Some words may have taken power over you—thoughts of not feeling valued or loved or worth time and energy. If someone in your life has told you something that does not line up with what God says about you, then you have to choose to break that verbal curse. These words may have even been spoken from well-meaning and loving people with the intent to help. But if those words are not biblical, it is time to break free from the lies and death spoken over you.

One time, I had a couple in my office who wanted to discuss the husband's anger outbursts and struggles with his temper. I asked questions to determine how long the husband had been angry and what the root problem was. He reported that he'd had issues controlling his anger for as long as he could remember, and it was now coming out in his marriage. He said, "I remember stories told over and over that my mom had to buy a book on how to parent an angry child."

"How many times have you been told that story?" I asked.

The once stoic man began to sob. "Too many times."

"I do not see an angry person in front of me," I said. "I see a person who struggles to express his emotions and feels helpless." I encouraged him to break the curse that he was an angry person and not to live in that identity. I encouraged him and his wife to speak out loud that he is not an angry person and can express himself.

Many times, words that others have spoken about us take control of our minds, and we begin to live as if that were our identity. We need to take those thoughts captive (2 Cor. 10:5) and fix our eyes on Jesus as the lifter of our head (Ps. 3:3).

If others have spoken curses and lies over your life, you have the power in God to break free from them.

Don't believe them. Call them as they are: curses meant to destroy your life. Remember, *"A thief comes only to steal and to kill and to destroy"* (John 10:10), and words have the power to do all of those things. The devil is crafty; he uses people who love us to deliver some of these devastating blows. Forgive those who have spoken the words and then change the words. Never contribute to destruction by speaking poorly of someone else—or yourself. Speak love and life over them and be cautious of your words. Through Christ you can break curses and destruction. Jesus came to give you life and to have it more abundantly (John 10:10).

Speak Life to Yourself

We also need to be aware of the words that we speak to ourselves, words that originate in our own minds and not from others. If we are speaking negative situations and bad things over our lives, then why should we be surprised when they happen? When you have that day you feel is going to be a long and difficult day, instead of saying, "Today is going to be exhausting and draining," say, "The Lord is going to sustain me today and give me the energy I need to thrive today. Even though I may be tired, I will have supernatural energy to operate from the gifts and the love of being an heir of Christ."

> *And the peace of God, which surpasses every thought, will guard your hearts and your minds in Christ Jesus. Finally brothers, whatever is true, whatever is honorable, whatever is just, whatever is pure, whatever is lovely, whatever is commendable—if there is any moral excellence and if there is any praise—dwell on these*

things. Do what you have learned and received and heard and seen in me, and the God of peace will be with you.

Phil. 4:7–9

Those are the guidelines for biblical, life-giving thoughts. If we focus on loving ourselves and others through the words that are spoken over us in God's Word, then we can expect the peace of God to follow us. When we speak negative words over our lives and spouses, we are doing the opposite of what God wants us to do.

If I speak death over my wife, then I have to be very careful of my own life because that is dangerously close to attacking God's anointed. You're not going to die if you say something negative, but you are breaking God's command to love people. Our words carry power, and you alone must choose what to do with that power. Those who are in Christ Jesus have an anointing over their lives; we are called to speak life into the fire and help it spread, not to quash it or extinguish the flame.

One Thing

Kids are awesome and joyous and fun, but they're also a lot of work! For the first year of my kids' lives, my wife and I both worked full-time jobs at home. She worked from home three days a week; I stayed home the two days she went into the office. A lot of that first year is a blur now since I started full-time counseling and became a dad of twins all within a week. I gained an even deeper and more profound respect for what homemakers do every day. They don't get days off. They work all day, every day.

Our lives have changed some since then; my wife no longer works at that job. Now she does creative freelance work and moms two active toddlers, all at home while I go into the office every day. But I'll never forget what it's like staying at home with two energetic kids. I have a ton of respect for what my wife does.

Hannah and I make a habit of letting each other know how we can serve one another frequently. I want her to know that serving her and loving her well are on my radar.

She also asks how she can serve me. I prefer a relatively neat house when I come home. As I mentioned earlier, I work late nights several days a week. There have been times when I come home and the house looks like a tornado landed, stayed around awhile, and then left just as I was pulling in the driveway. Here is a moment in which I can choose what I want to speak into my wife. Do I want to remind her of how much she has failed today? Or do I speak life into her?

You only need one thing. Can you find one thing to pull out and love on? Honestly, my wife knows that the house is a mess and doesn't need me to tell her. We are our toughest critics, and she's probably already overwhelmed. But what if I can show her some empathy and love in the midst of the chaos? I can say, "Babe, it looks like you've had a tough day. How can I help?"

Again, she knows the house is a disaster. But she needs an empathetic word and encouragement that I love her and appreciate her and still choose her over a clean house. When you can love on your spouse and speak kindness and love in the midst of struggles, you will become closer than you ever have before. You get to see each other's junk and brokenness and show that you love each other just as you are.

"A spouse needs your kind words and empathy first, not your judgement, criticism, and correction."

As the old saying goes "If you can't say something nice, then don't say it at all." A spouse needs your kind words and empathy first, not your judgment, criticism, and correction.

Watch Your Shame

Shame on you are words we've all heard growing up that can be damaging to the soul. Christ did not come so that you can live in shame; he came so you can be free and live in freedom! You have a mandate to pour into your spouse and kids. Be very careful of what comes out of your mouth. Parents, watch what you speak and declare over your kids. Shame is powerful.

One of my favorite verses in the Bible is Genesis 2:25: *"Both the man and his wife were naked, yet felt no shame."* I love this verse because I cannot imagine a world without shame. They were in their most vulnerable state, yet they felt no shame. This verse isn't really about nudity; it's about being completely known. As Kramer on *Seinfeld* would say, "They're all out there, Jer!" And they were loving it.

We all have things that can create shame in our lives. It could be a deep, dark sin that nobody knows about. It could be your lack of resources. It could be something that was done to you that you had no control over such as abuse or trauma. Shame can be an identity, but you must release yourself from the pain of the past. It's easy to live in the shame that we feel. It makes sense why we would want to cover that up and not be authentic and real. The problem is that, in order to be close and connected and moving toward Christ in our relationships, we have to continue to fight through our shame and be all that God has designed us for. If shame is something that has a hold of your life, then please seek additional resources to help you break the chains that are holding you back. I will put a couple of resources in the appendix at the end of this book.

CHAPTER 5

In Our Home We Laugh Loudly

"A day without laughter is a day wasted."
—Charlie Chaplin

When was the last time you belly laughed with your spouse? You know the laugh I'm talking about—the one that makes your stomach hurt and your bladder weak. Marriage should be fun. I hope you have many inside jokes that only you and your spouse understand.

We plan fun dates with one another, time in which we just act silly and enjoy one another. We play a game we made up called elbow ball. We throw and catch a beach ball across the room using just our elbows. Or we throw grapes into each other's mouths from a faraway distance.

(Apparently, silly throwing games really get us in a jovial mood.) It doesn't matter the activity that you choose to laugh about or have fun with—just get creative and enjoy one another.

Research has even stated that it is easier to smile than it is to frown. It literally takes more muscles in your face to show your grumpy face than it does to exercise your smiley side. Earlier this evening, my wife was in a bit of a funk, and I asked her to genuinely smile for 15 seconds. She began laughing during the process due to the awkwardness it takes to hold a smile for that long. I can't tell you how many inside jokes we have that will crack both of us up at the very mention of them. We have a face that we make called the "stink-eye face" or voices that we make up with certain lines that made us laugh the moment those inside jokes were created. We have joke after joke, and thankfully our list keeps growing. The reason our laughing and jokes keep continuing is that we spend time with one another. We get to know each other's worlds. When you smile, no matter the circumstance, it changes your mood by its very nature.

Let's do an exercise right now: Smile the biggest grin you have ever done, and then hold it for 15 seconds just like my wife did. Ready . . . Set . . . Smile.

If you smiled your big, goofy, and joyous smile for 15 seconds, then by the very science of what smiles do, no matter how you were feeling prior to your smile, you should feel slightly better than before you flashed your pearly whites.

PhD

Do you remember what it was like when you first started dating your spouse? Maybe you are in that place now, feeling butterflies right before a date. You go on your date and want nothing more than to get to know this person. It's almost like an interview, and you're applying for the position of boyfriend or girlfriend. You're learning about one another's likes and dislikes and figuring out what makes this person tick.

I know many people date for the sake of dating, but dating should have a purpose. If you're dating someone because you're tired of being lonely, then you're dating for the wrong reason. Even in a relationship you can find yourself lonely because you don't learn how to be a whole person in a dating relationship. Marriage is when two whole people come together and make a greater whole. Two whole people become one; they are not two halves equaling one. Dating helps you determine if you can possibly marry the person one day. Once you've passed the extensive interview process, you can move forward.

For our first date, Hannah and I ate at Pei Wei for dinner and then browsed through Barnes and Noble. (Note: Guys, learn to love and enjoy this process because shopping and browsing with your spouse definitely does not end after you say, "I do.")

At Pei Wei, I sat facing the kitchen. If you've ever been to Pei Wei, the kitchen is a constant fire show. I tried to listen to my date pour her heart out and interview me, but my eyes were drawn to the large flames in the background. She probably thought I had ADHD or was a really bad listener. Neither are true, for the record, but the flames were distracting. Thankfully, we laughed about it and talked about it even then. I think she even told me once that she could see the flames through my eyes. What a beautiful statement. She had looked so intently into my eyes that she could see the reflection of the flames. I hope we never lose that intensity, the desire to stare at one another with complete focus and attention to detail. She was trying to see into my soul. We enjoyed dating, and eventually our engagement, and now marriage.

We do a good job of fishing and learning about our spouses in the first stages of a relationship, but then so many of us stop the dating process. We've reeled them in, and the catch is a keeper. But unlike the catch of the day, your spouse is always on the line, either swimming toward you, with you, or away from you. Keep going after them. Keep learning what makes your spouse tick. You should never stop dating, learning, and growing together.

> "But unlike the catch of the day, your spouse is always on the line, either swimming toward you, with you, or away from you. Keep going after them. Keep learning what makes your spouse tick. You should never stop dating, learning, and growing together."

We should have a PhD in the person we have chosen to share our lives with. I have my master's degree, have strongly considered getting my PhD, and I know what it takes in order to get these accolades. It takes a lot of time, energy, work, and dedication. I think we should have the same mentality with our spouses. You should be 90 years old and still learning about one another (not just the 70 that Ed Sheeran states in his great song "Thinking Out Loud," but he is on the right track).

It's more difficult to date now that we have kids, but we cannot forget to date one another. If you don't have kids and don't go on date nights regularly, then look at your calendar with your spouse and plan your next date as soon as possible. They should occur frequently, regardless of your family or financial circumstances. I ask every couple that sees me to go on a date for $20 or less. That could be as simple as cooking a meal together after you put the kids to bed! Dessert on the back patio feels different when you're doing it with purpose. Be creative and intentional with your date. The date should be more about the quality of the date than the quantity of what we spend because the purpose is to fall more in love with one another. On that note, I should mention that dates are not for talking about the complexities of doing life together — not work, money, or kids. Why? Because, as married couples who do life together, those are life discussions we have regardless of whether or not we go on a date. They are off limits on date night.

We laugh a lot. We have family dance parties at least once a week. My wife and kids probably have them four or five nights a week. They happen regularly because they are a fun exercise and get us all to laugh. We have a friend who reminded us that the phrase "Ha" is actually short for the Hebrew word Hallelujah. So when we say, "Ha," we're actually inviting God into our praise. I think God smiles and laughs with us, not at us. That is an important difference. God does not mock you when you mess up or struggle. He is overjoyed when we love him and his people well. He takes delight in the nuances of his creations because he has created us all to be unique and beautiful. I don't always feel happy or excited, and in those times I have to remind myself to smile and laugh. I'm not denying my circumstances, only laughing in spite of the circumstances. This isn't to make light of difficulties or struggles. Just remember that we don't get our sole source of happiness from external circumstances. When I remember to keep God at the top, I can laugh when days are good or bad because my joy comes from him.

When marriage becomes all about the rituals and daily routine, then we have lost a key element that makes marriage so enjoyable. So crank up the music and have a dance party because it's time to get your praise and laughter on!

CHAPTER 6

In Our Home We Are Honest

"Anyone who doesn't take truth seriously in small matters cannot be trusted in larger ones either."

— Albert Einstein

My parents took my wife and me, along with my sister and brother-in-law, to Disney World and Universal Studios in Florida before any of us had kids. We had so much fun on this trip that Hannah and I both decided to go back with our kids when they are older.

While we were on that trip, we went on *The Pirates of the Caribbean* ride. During this attraction, you stand in a large group and basically watch simulated bombs go off between two ships right in front of you. It's not my favorite attraction, but it's one I will never forget because of the oath they make you take prior to the start of the event.

While you wait outside in the blistering heat, a cast member enthusiastically explains what's about to happen. At the end of his speech, he tells everyone to raise a hand and repeat an oath after him. The end of the oath states, "So help me Davy Jones." It makes sense because Davy Jones is a part of *The Pirates of the Caribbean* theme, and he wanted us to make a promise. The problem was that I did not hear him say *Davy Jones*. I misunderstood and thought he said "tell the jokes." So, I loudly and proudly repeated, "So help me tell the jokes!" My family and I started laughing so hard at my misunderstanding, and it has been a running joke in our family ever since.

In our marriage, we must also take the oath to be honest and tell the truth, not because a tour guide makes us repeat it, but because honesty creates a safe environment.

Tell Truths

Here's a funny story. When we were coming up with our family rules, we wrote them down on a notepad before my wife put them permanently on the sign. We originally wrote down *We Tell the Truth*. When she painted it on the sign, she ran out of room after the word *Tell*, so she wrote *We Tell Truths*. We laughed about it, but we couldn't leave it. She had to sand the board clean, restain it, and come up with the shorter, *We Are Honest*.

Honesty is such an important quality in a marriage, and when trust is broken it takes a lot to restore it. When I was in seventh grade, we had to memorize vocabulary words with their definitions, and to this day I remember the definition that they provided us for the word *integrity*: honesty, uprightness, and sincerity.

During my time in Colorado, I came up with what at the time I thought were the three keys to a successful marriage. They had this incredible and catchy title called *Aaron's Three Things*. Great title, right? It took me quite awhile to come up with something that had such a nice ring to it. Those three things have cultivated and grown since then, but they still assume that you are pursuing God with a complete abandon. The first is honesty—complete honesty, telling the whole truth and holding nothing back.

Sometimes we hold back pieces of the truth out of fear: If my husband really knows how depressed I am, he will think differently about me. If my wife knows that I have struggled with lust, she will shame me, and I don't want her to stop loving me or leave me. But marriages must be real, sharing ugly truths with each other rather than hiding behind pain or hurt.

This concept came to me when I was talking to Hannah on the phone and somehow my feelings got hurt. Hannah asked me later if she had hurt my feelings, and I was honest and said that she had, but not completely honest. I had held back that I was still hurt. So I started over, this time admitting that I was still hurt and needed to talk about it.

We should not withhold truth, even painful truth, from our spouses. When people are ashamed of their sin or a painful truth, rather than express it, they tend to live in secret. But the only way to live as God has called us to—to live freely—is to be honest. The Bible says *"where the spirit of the Lord is, there is freedom"* (2 Cor. 3:17).

Freedom! Christ came into the world and died so that we can experience freedom. We can't live in freedom in life or in marriage without being honest and real.

I don't like the term "white lies." Truth is truth. Maybe you feel like Jack Nicholson in *A Few Good Men*—that your spouse can't handle the truth. But you don't get to decide what your spouse can and can't handle. You have to trust God to take care of your spouse and their emotions more than you ever could. We may want to cover up areas of our lives to protect our spouses, but God has called us to live marriage as in Genesis 2:25: fully known and without shame. We need to be honest and upfront, trusting God to uphold both us and our spouses. When I hold back information from my wife, I'm not allowing God to do his job of taking care of me *and* Hannah.

> "You have to trust God to take care of your spouse and their emotions more than you ever could."

Maybe you grew up in a home in which you were punished when you did things wrong. Maybe you were physically beaten or verbally reprimanded every time you made an error. You may have taught yourself that you would rather your parents not know what you were doing to avoid consequences. You learned to cover things up, to avoid losing the love and attention you craved. But it's vital to overcome this, to reteach yourself to be fully honest with yourself and others. Something powerful happens when you learn to be honest about your faults and struggles and continue to fight and push forward.

Unfortunately, I see a lot of couples in counseling who suffer from a spouse who's had an affair. Many times the affair has already been discovered prior to seeing me. *Discovered.* That's usually the way it happens. Someone has hidden his or her sin, just like David did with Bathsheba. David wanted to hide his adultery and sin. Who knows what would have happened to him if the Lord had not revealed his sin to Nathan, who exposed him? Thank God for graciously allowing our sin to come into the light. What we try to keep in the dark, God will mercifully bring to light. Research states that people can handle a lot of pain at once, but they have a hard time processing and dealing with repeated pain. If someone having an affair or addiction confesses the issue in full disclosure rather than bits and pieces, the healing process is much easier. It is never easy but the little truth here and there followed by repeated lies is even more devastating. Many times, when I have talked with the spouses of those who have had an affair or an addiction, they are hurt by the act itself but usually the deceit and the lies hurt them even more. When little pieces of the truth come out, the spouse may begin to wonder if trust will ever be restored.

> "What we try to keep in the dark, God will mercifully bring to light."

If you have been dishonest or deceitful toward your spouse, begin today to live in complete honesty. Let them know that you have some things to say that won't be easy to say or hear, but you want to express your heart and be fully known.

Sit with the Pain

As a general rule, our society doesn't know what do with other people's pain. Pain makes us uncomfortable, and we'd rather be happy and content, smiling and singing *We Are the World*. The avoidance of pain became very clear to me when someone I know lost a loved one to suicide. People didn't know how to respond, so instead, they ostracized this friend.

We want to relate to others in conversation because it makes us feel that we have something to contribute. When someone you know is having a baby, they make the announcement and tell everyone the name they have chosen, let's say Gerald. Inevitably people say things like, "My uncle's name is Gerald," or "I knew a guy in school named Gerald," because they want to relate. The problem is that they took that moment and made it about themselves. There are times when relating can be useful, but it shouldn't be our default answer because, when we can't relate, we don't know what to do. The problem with pain is that we often can't relate.

We can't relate to others' pain all the time. Each person's pain is unique, and even if you have experienced something similar, you may have responded differently. We need to learn how to sit with the pain. Pain is uncomfortable and awkward. Suicide, death, infertility, divorce—these topics tend to make us feel uncomfortable, but it's okay to feel uncomfortable. We don't always have to know what to say in order to have a conversation with someone. We can't avoid conversations out of fear of discomfort.

Just recently, my friend lost his wife shortly after the birth of their first son. They had known each other for years before falling in love, getting married, and deciding to start a family. But tragically, just a couple of months after giving birth she became ill and passed away. I saw him for the first time a few months afterward. I sat with him and asked how he was doing. He gave the obligatory, "Hanging in there."

"How are you really doing?" I asked. We then had a conversation about life, his pain, his trust in God even in the sadness. He said that he had not even had time to grieve because he'd been so busy adjusting to fatherhood. At the end of the conversation, he thanked me for listening, letting him be real rather than asking him to put on the mask that most people wanted him to wear.

For my wife's 30th birthday, I asked her friends to write her notes letting her know how much they loved and appreciated her. I got emotional several times as I read them. One friend stated that Hannah was the only person in her life who asked how she was doing and really wanted to know the answer to the question. Let us be people who ask about the well-being of others and genuinely listen.

We All Have the Potential

We live in a world that tells you to suck it up and keep going. You can't sit around and cry about things that have happened in your life; you have to get up and dust yourself off! Picture a five-year-old playing tee ball. He hits the ball and runs—to third base. He finally figures out which way to run, and then trips and falls halfway to first base. You don't run onto the field to dote: "You poor guy, I bet that really hurt your knee. If you need to cry a little bit before you get back up, then that's okay!" No, instead you graciously yell from the bleachers, "Get up, buddy; dust off. You're all good."

Recently, my family and I were eating dinner at Torchy's Tacos, which is an awesome little taco shop that started in Austin and has now moved its way to a few other cities, including our hometown, Houston. We were eating outside on a lovely 75-degree day in November, enjoying our chips and queso, when suddenly a car behind us honked rather loudly. Someone was looking for her car and pushed the panic button, blaring the horn right behind my three-year-old son. All of us jumped, but my son was very startled. He tried to be brave and went to reach for another chip and queso, but it was obvious to Hannah and me that he was upset. Tears welled in his eyes, but he felt as if he couldn't cry because everyone else carried on as normal. Hannah went over to him and picked him up and assured him that it was okay to be sad. The moment she said those words he began to cry and let his tears flow freely. His mother had assured him that it was okay to be sad and to cry and that it had scared her a little too. Then he cried with the assurance of his mother's love. He needed permission to cry. When Hannah pulled him close and provided that safety net of support, he could be fully toddler and fully man at only three years old by expressing himself freely, and that was the bravest thing he could do. I wish we could all be so free with our emotions and vulnerabilities. Many times, people need to know that it's okay not to have it all together all the time. It's okay to be scared or frightened or sad. What we have to do is provide that safe place to let them express what they are feeling.

Many people struggle showing emotion, but we all have it. In fact research shows that we have seven basic, universal emotions: fear, joy, surprise, sadness, anger, disgust, and contempt. If you've ever seen the movie *Inside Out* by Pixar, you have a general idea about how emotions can play a large part of our lives. I highly encourage this film because it is very well done and does a great job of explaining all the emotions needed to work together in order to operate in full potential. So if we have these basic emotions, why do we struggle showing them or expressing them? The answer depends on the person. Maybe because we're taught that "there's no crying in baseball." We think that emotions or pain equal weakness. We recognize that crying doesn't fix the situation. Some people stuff their own feelings or emotions inside in order to survive. They just had to stuff it inside in order to keep on going. Sometimes it is appropriate to do so. We can't cry and mope around all day, but that doesn't mean that we should never address it or talk about it. It's okay to talk about pain and difficult situations—and it's necessary. How did Jesus respond when there was pain?

Jesus Wept

Jesus had several friends. Some of his closest friends were Mary, Martha, and Lazarus. He loved these people. Mary sat at his feet and listened while Martha worked hard to make the house presentable for him. But one day, Lazarus got sick. They thought it was all good because they were close friends with Jesus. They had faith that Jesus could not only heal their brother, but would. Many times in our lives I wonder if we have lost the passion and faith that they had in the Bible. We pray for healing but do we really believe we are going to be healed? Faith, rise up!

So, they sent a message to Jesus that their brother was dying. Jesus got the message but did not come. He stayed where he was and went about his business as usual. The disciples asked Jesus about the situation, and Jesus said that it was better for them that he was not there and that meant Lazarus was going to die. That had to be confusing. I can just hear Peter or Thomas saying, "But, Jesus, you love this guy. Let's go heal him!" By the time Jesus got to the house, Lazarus was dead. He had been dead for four days!

Many times in our lives God does not show up when we want him to. I heard once that we live in a microwave world and serve a crockpot God. God's timing is not our timing. We have to remain faithful and steadfast even in the waiting when we feel like God is lacking an answer for us. However, you never know when your "day four" is coming.

So Jesus arrived, and Mary came to him. She asked him where he was and said that if he had been there, her brother would not have died. She knew that Jesus could heal, and I imagine she was a little annoyed that He arrived late. Then Jesus asked to see the grave, and when he arrived to the tomb, he wept (John 11:35).

Wept! The word here does not mean he had a few tears dripping down his face like I do when watching *The Notebook*. No, the word here describes a wailing. He cried so loudly that others around him murmured, "Man, he must have really loved this Lazarus guy." Now, if you know the end of the story, then you know that Jesus is about to blow everybody's mind and raise Lazarus from the dead. So here is my question: If Jesus knew he was about to raise Lazarus from the dead and knew that in just a few minutes they would be fellowshipping again, then why did he weep?

I believe Jesus cried for two reasons. First, I think he was crying over death itself. He was angered and saddened that death had dominion over the world. God created us to live forever, but then sin entered the world and death came roaring in. I think this is part of the reason we all have such a hard time dealing with and processing death. We were not meant to experience it.

The second reason is that even though he was about to raise Lazarus from the dead, he did not negate the pain that Mary and Martha had for losing their brother. Jesus cried *with* them. He sat there and grieved with them. When we experience pain or trauma, we live in a world that tells us to keep on going—to pick yourself up by your bootstraps and press on. However, that is not how Jesus himself responded. He cries. Jesus is crying with you as you experience the loss of a loved one, the struggles of depression or anxiety, the abuse you've suffered. He cries with you because it's not okay. He is deeply pained that you are experiencing so much pain and hurt. He loves you and knows what you are going through. He didn't tell Mary and Martha, "Suck it up! What's wrong with you ladies crying over such a small thing? I've got this. I am God." He doesn't tell them to shut down their feelings or emotions. In fact, he joins them and cries with them. One of the best things we can do for people experiencing pain is to create space to sit and cry with them.

But I Want to Fix It

As I write this chapter, I'm sitting in a cabin in the mountains in Colorado Springs. It is gorgeous up here, and right now it's 55 degrees. It is the end of October, and the leaves are a lovely red and orange, and I could stare at them all day long.

I'm on a retreat for Foster/Adoptive dads. As foster or adoptive parents, we experience something that others can't relate to. We have pain and hurt and joy and trauma and stuff that others have a hard time understanding. I have had several conversations with dads here who are experiencing tremendous pain. This retreat has provided an opportunity to be real with our hurts and our insecurities about the calling that God has placed on our lives to be foster and adoptive parents. It is beautiful, but it is also messy. One gentleman shared that as he's going through trials with his adopted teenage children, someone close to him has questioned why he doesn't retract or withdraw on the adoption. As an adoptive parent, this is heartbreaking and unfathomable. The real issue is that the person who said this was really trying to help, trying to provide relief to a hard situation. However, this was a horrible solution because it doesn't work that way. When you've gone through the adoption process, those children are your kids. I could write a whole dissertation on this and really express my hurt and anger over such conversations, but I won't. This person was not trying to be malicious or mean. This gentleman then said something that I wish everyone would understand: he didn't need advice, just a listening ear for him to express his vulnerabilities, struggles, and insecurities. Just listening to people and empathizing with their pain is helping. It is a stereotype that men just want to help fix a problem, but men need to know that listening to their spouses talk about their hard day or difficult time without trying to solve anything is helping. They need to sit with their spouses and validate their spouses' feelings with an empathetic ear. This could radically change conversations.

When we come clean and are honest with our past hurts and struggles, we can experience what it's like to sit with pain. The truth may hurt, but the Bible also says that truth will set you free (John 8:32). Be honest. Be real. Be true. And don't negate or shut down others' pain. Sit with the pain, even if you are the one who caused it.

CHAPTER 7

In Our Home We Are Thankful

"Silent gratitude isn't very much to anyone."
—Gertrude Stein

D id you know that if you live in the United States you are one of the wealthiest people in the world? In fact, a majority of American households are among the top one percent of the wealthiest people in the world. I have heard varying numbers on this percentage, but the truth is that Americans are very privileged people.[1] Talk about perspective. When I'm struggling to pay bills and to make our payments for the month, I have to remember to be thankful for what I have. Honestly, if my list of needs and wants are longer than my list of things I'm thankful for, then I have a real problem. I have lost perspective. I have lost my sense of what it means to live in thankfulness and gratefulness.

It is easy to see what we want more of. We should make our requests known to the Lord. The Bible says to knock and keep on knocking (Matt. 7:7, Luke 11:9). But, God wants to be so much more to me than my Santa Claus in the sky. He wants to sit with me and love me. He wants to enjoy me as part of his creation. He is my daddy.

I don't know what kind of father you had. Maybe you lost your father or never knew him. Maybe your father was an authoritarian or an absent figure and you can't process what I mean when I say that God is your Abba Father. God never leaves you nor forsakes you (Deut. 31:6). Father God knows you and cares about you more than you can imagine. Abba Father is a name that is used for God showing his intimate relationship in knowing us. Abba Father means God is your daddy.

As I mentioned, my wife has the lovely and difficult task of loving and being with our kids on a daily basis. She doesn't get a break from her job; it continues whether or not she needs a breather. Many times when I come home late at night, the kids are winding down and starting to get ready for bed. If you have kids, then you know that the nighttime routine may be better known as "the witching hour." Something happens to kids when the sun goes down. It's almost as if the fairy godmother from *Cinderella* has put a spell on them that expires at sunset. Despite these moments of parental frustration and bliss, I love coming home from work to be with my wife and kids.

Most days when I come home from work, despite whatever shenanigans they've pulled three seconds before I walk in the door, my kids scream, "Daddy!" and come running at full sprint into my arms. It is by far the best part of my day. When they see their daddy and run to me, it makes my heart swell. On the rare days that they do not come running with glee, it saddens me. The question that haunts me is not, "do I treat God like that?" but, "how often do I treat God like that?"

How often do I just come to God asking for things and making requests? How often do I get so busy in my own world and my own witching hour that I neglect to look my daddy in the face? One summer, I spoke on marriage and family at a church's family camp. We spent a week at the camp, which is summer camp for the whole family. We had two beds in our room, so Hannah and I each shared a bed with a child. My daughter and I shared the same bed, and every night she held my face and just stared at me. She knows my face. She knows the curves on my face and the length of my beard hairs and when I shave. She knows my face because she spends a lot of time looking at it and memorizing it. It's a security as well as comfort for her. I think one of the things God loves most is when we come and just sit in his presence. I love to spend time with my kids and give them hugs and kisses. I love to wrap them in my arms and squeeze them. I love to tickle them and make them smile. I love to be in their presence. I love meeting their requests too, but if all they ever did was make requests, then I wouldn't be as eager to meet those needs. My kids love me and want to spend time with me, regardless that I provide their food and housing. Let's face it: they are three. They have no idea what it takes to provide for them—the nights I spend working late hours and pouring into others in order to help others but also them. They do not know what Hannah and I do for them, but they do care about us. Remember, they want us more than *anything else.*

Thankful to God First

God loves me no matter what I do to provide for my kids or my wife. His love is unconditional. If I've had a bad day or I'm stressed out with work or life's demands, he wants nothing more than to hold me and let me feel his love. I'm thankful he loves me despite my junk. I am thankful that I do not have to be perfect in order to feel his love. I am thankful that his grace covers me and that I can rest in the shadows of the almighty and let him sing and dance over me. Jared Anderson wrote a song called "Amazed" based on Zephaniah 3:17[2]: "*Yahweh your God is among you, a warrior who saves. He will rejoice over you with gladness. He will bring you quietness with His love. He will delight in you with shouts of joy.*" One of the lines of this song says "You dance over me while I am unaware." I love this picture of God dancing and singing over me even when I am focused on me and unaware of his presence and gaze. I am thankful to God first because, if I forget that love and desire and sacrifice he makes for me, then it is easy to get focused on my own desires. I want to "Enter his gates with thanksgiving and his courts with praise" (Ps. 100:4). I want to lead with a thank you. If I am not first thankful for what God has done for me and for the overwhelming love he has for me, then I cannot fully express thankfulness to others. Our God is such a good father. I love the Housefires's song "Good Good Father." You may have thought that was a Chris Tomlin song, but Housefires did it first. They are an amazing and powerful Christian band. If you're not familiar with them, then it's time to get you acquainted. Powerful. Most of the time I am writing, I have Housefires on Pandora, jamming and worshiping as I write. "Good Good Father" has powerful lyrics that speak about how good God is as a father. I know many people who have struggled with this song because of feelings toward their own father; but if we could redefine what it means to be a father, then we may just be on the path toward leaning into his love and heart for you.

He loves us so much! I have heard some say that if God has a refrigerator then your picture would be on it. Maybe this is cheesy, but I do love the intentionality that it shows about our God caring about every aspect of our lives and wanting nothing more than to love on you and help you look more like him. My kids bring home artwork from Sunday school every single week. They sometimes bring three or four pieces home each week! I'm so thankful for teachers loving my kids well and teaching them about God, but what am I supposed to do with all of these Picassos? I know if I were the perfect father then I would hang them on my refrigerator or put them in a keepsake box of treasures. But 99 percent of them end up in the trash. I love my kids, and I love the artwork they do, but if I put them all on the refrigerator, I'd have to buy about 10 refrigerators a year to keep up with their masterpieces. I'm so thankful that God does not get tired of me or the artwork that I present to him. He puts my picture on the refrigerator and thinks of me at all times. And he does the same thing for you.

If I don't remember how much I have to be thankful for from God and all he has done for me, then I will never be able to show the full extent of thankfulness to my wife and kids or even my friends. I didn't do anything to earn the love of God. He loves me because he created me and I am his. I am thankful for something I didn't even have to pay for. Christ died for me even before I said I loved him or was even aware of his presence. I received it free of cost. If I received it for free, then it makes it a lot easier to give it away to others. As the American evangelist Billy Graham stated, "A spirit of thankfulness is one of the most distinctive marks of a Christian whose heart is attuned to the Lord. Thank God in the midst of trials and every persecution."[3] So now that you have the premise that you have to be thankful to God and all that he is to you in your life, how do you take that next step and be thankful for your family and your spouse?

> "If I don't remember how much I have to be thankful for from God and all he has done for me, then I will never be able to show the full extent of thankfulness to my wife and kids or even my friends."

Great question. It starts with a simple thank you. Saying thank you is not a one-time event. I want to create a culture of appreciation in our home. I may feel thankful and appreciative toward my wife, but if I do not verbalize my appreciation and thankfulness, she has no idea how I am feeling. Gary Chapman wrote a book called *The Five Love Languages*.[4] In his book, he states that there are really five ways that most people feel loved, and we tend to show the same type of love to others that we desire for ourselves. For example, if quality time is my primary love language, then when I try to show Hannah love, I may want to spend quality time with her, because that is what

I would prefer. This works well if you and your wife speak the same love language. If you don't, then your hard work isn't as meaningful to them as it is to you. It's heartbreaking when you're attempting to show love but missing what's needed.

Another of these five love languages is words of affirmation. Whether or not words of affirmation is your love language, stating appreciation and affirming one another is always beneficial and life-giving. So thank your spouse for hard work and diligence, and honesty and integrity. Thank your spouse for going to the grocery store and shopping for the family, for sacrificing time and self. Thank your spouse for loving you. Thank your spouse for who they are. Praise them for their character and not just their achievements. Show them gratitude over and over again.

What Is Love?

I briefly mentioned the concept of love earlier, but it's time to take that subject further and get real. There are a few things that really bother me when it comes to counseling. One of these things is when people tell me they don't *feel* that they love their spouses anymore. They've lost that loving feeling, as the song goes. But love cannot and should not be based on how a person is feeling because married love is not conditional.

Old School DC Talk

There are many song references that discuss this idea that love is more than we thought it was when we first got married. DC Talk was a Christian band from the '90s. Any '90s kid who grew up with Christian music knows of DC

Talk. The band had numerous songs that we all rocked out to in youth group: "Jesus Freak," "Time Is Ticking Away," "Free at Last," and they did a remake of "Lean on Me." One of my favorite songs by DC Talk is "Luv Is a Verb."[5] Have you ever asked someone what being in love is or what love is? The answers I hear are fascinating:

"It feels like butterflies in my stomach."

"I feel the feels all over when I am around her."

"It just feels so good to be around him."

"He makes me feel special and cared for."

"She treats me better than anyone ever has."

"She is beautiful inside and out."

"Love is that wonderful feeling that makes it feel like Christmas all year round."

Wait a second. Love makes it feel like Christmas all year round and makes you have butterflies? No wonder so many people are calling it quits when that *feeling* is no longer what drives them! If love were really that fickle and shallow, then what is the point? As another great band, Boston, would say, love is "More Than a Feeling." It has to be. We have to base our love on more than just how we are feeling at a given moment.

> "We have to base our love on more than just how we are feeling at a given moment."

Love Is an Act of Faith

I remember one of our first fights very clearly. Let me restate that: I remember the outcome of our first fight clearly. (I have no clue what the actual argument was about.) We were talking, and then the talking felt sour in my mouth, quickly becoming rancid and unhealthy.

You know the feeling. The feeling that a conversation has now come really close to becoming an argument. You now have a decision to make. Are you going to continue the argument, or take a breather? The smart move is to take breather and come back to it, but we did not. We said some more words that were difficult to hear—not horrible, but not ones that we were proud of either. After the conversation, I felt ill—the nauseating feeling of being further apart and wondering what in the world just happened. I started to sulk and feel sorry for myself when I remembered the three things I learned in Colorado.

The first is something we've already covered in this book: honesty versus complete honesty. The second is to keep small things small. In my years as a therapist, I have concluded that many marriages don't end over single events, except for possibly a traumatic event like an affair or abuse. A majority of marriages end because of many small things building up. There are two ways to get a bruise. You can have one solid blow that creates the bruise or small repeated pokes in the same spot. The effect is still the same—pain. I wanted to learn how to keep a small thing small and attempt to reconcile the argument before it escalated. I was trying to avoid statements beginning with *you never* or *you always*. I wanted to make small adjustments in our relationship and address the small issues or "foxes" as the Bible would call them (Song of Sol. 2:15). You have to get rid of the small foxes in your yard, or the whole garden will be destroyed.

After this argument, however, I walked away, breathing heavily, feeling that my wife had wronged me. I knew that I could keep small things small or let this one fester, and I decided to lay down my pride and my pain to serve her through it.

My wife loves massages from me at any time of the day, so although the air was still tense from our argument, I gave her one. At first she was confused. Had I lost my marbles? I explained to her that she was more important than our argument; my love and our relationship was more important than anything. I chose us instead of my pain and hurt, acting out my love in faith. I didn't feel loving at that moment, but I chose to love her anyway. Love is an action, a verb.

I know what you're thinking: "Aaron, I don't know if I can do that. What if my spouse never loves me in faith, and here I am laying my life down and getting nothing in return?" I think this is a valid question, but it's one you must refuse to ask yourself. This question doesn't lead to a heart change or help you do your job as a spouse. The Bible says in Ephesians 5:25 that husbands are supposed to love their wives as Jesus did when he laid down his life for her. My job is to lay my life down and serve my wife, to love her even when I feel hurt. Jesus died for us in the midst of being treated unfairly. He loves us as a choice, not because of how we treat him. I am supposed to love my wife even when she does not love me well.

> "I don't get to choose when I want to lay my life down for her. I vowed to do it all the time. If I choose to love her according to her behaviors or merits, then my love is conditional and manipulative."

God has called us to love our spouses and leave the rest to him. If I only love my wife when she treats me well or loves me right, then I'll end up bitter and resentful. I don't get to choose when I want to lay my life down for her. I vowed to do it all the time.

If I choose to love her according to her behaviors or merits, then my love is conditional and manipulative. If I serve my wife only to be rewarded and praised, then my love is hypocritical. I cannot love her for what I get out of it. I have to love her even when I don't feel like it. Remember, the only thing we can choose to do is love our spouses well.

You may also argue that your marriage problems are not your fault. You may have married a legitimately difficult person to live with, but the truth is that you are both probably at fault in some way. You are probably not showing *perfect* Christlike love in every moment. Choose to look inwardly first and search your own heart before blaming your spouse for all the marital issues. I mentioned that men are supposed to lay their lives down for their wives. I think Paul does a good job in 1 Corinthians stating that love and sacrifice is a two way street. My friend Jerrell says that without love you're annoying; he bases this on 1 Corinthians 13:1. When I think of being annoying, I think of the scene in *Dumb and Dumber* when Floyd asks Harry what the most annoying sound in the world is. He then proceeds by making this obnoxious and ridiculous sound that still rings in my ears in the middle of some of my nightmares. Don't be annoying. Instead, choose love, and keep on giving those massages.

CHAPTER 8

In Our Home We Forgive – Part 1

"A happy marriage is the union of two good forgivers."

—Ruth Bell Graham

I was a good kid. Maybe my parents don't agree, but I have the microphone. I was a good kid, and I rarely got in trouble. I was sarcastic at times and talked a lot, but if my parents even threatened to get upset, I would tear up. I have a deep sense of people-pleasing, a negative trait since my purpose is to please God alone. However, as a child, I knew I didn't like it when I got in trouble because I didn't like people to be disappointed or angry with me.

My sister is four years younger than I am, but for most of our childhood, she was my best friend. We played with all sorts of toys together—Green Lantern, dinosaurs, and

Flash. We also had this little tiny blue guy that we called Lad. I'm not sure if that was his name, but we went with it. My sister and I have very different personalities, but we usually made it work. My parents told us that when my sister was a couple of years old, we would play and then my sister would pull my hair. (Remember, I don't have many hairs, so each one is precious to me.) She would pull my hair, and then *she* would start to cry. What a little stinker, right? Of course, my parents would come in, scold me for hurting my sister, and tell me to apologize. They finally caught on to her devious childhood ways and made her apologize to me. Unfortunately, my head never recovered, and I have since embraced being bald. They say that baldness comes from your mother's side of the family. My maternal grandfather has more hair on his head at 80 than I've ever had. Maybe they were wrong about where baldness comes from. Or maybe my poor head suffered so much trauma as a child that it never fully recovered. Thanks, sis.

I Don't Want to Fight

Conflict is inevitable. In fact, Dr. John Gottman, who has done countless research on couples and marriages, has concluded that 69 percent of marital conflict will not go away; it is perpetual.[1] So, if we recognize that we're going to have conflict or disagreements, we need to have conversations about those conflicts, or we're doing ourselves a disservice.

Couples use two extremes when it comes to conflict. The first is fighting and yelling. This is usually explosive and not very respectful, leading to hopelessness. This extreme typically ends the marriage or makes it miserable.

The second extreme is never fighting at all. At first glance, this couple may sound wonderful. But this causes couples to bottle up their frustrations until they're ready to explode and explosions are nasty (think the ghost from *Ghostbusters*).

Neither of these extremes is a successful recipe for marital bliss. Let's tackle both and why they are so destructive, and then look at a possible alternative.

The fighting and yelling couple fights all the time with a raging temper. They hold nothing back, going for it with their boxing gloves on. Sometimes, believe it or not, they may be fighting nonstop for religious reasons. They take the scripture literally that says, *"Don't let the sun go down on your anger"* (Eph. 4:26). They want to make sure they are doing the right thing by trying to figure it all out prior to calling it a night. If we take this verse literally, then we wouldn't fight past about 6 to 8 p.m., depending on where we are with daylight savings. That means we'd have to hash it out while the kids are still awake, and I'm fairly certain that's not what you really want to do. So Ephesians 4:26 doesn't sound literal, does it?

I think this verse is more about resentment. It's not about what time of day to have your arguments because, let's face it, most of our difficult topics come up at night because we're tired and cranky from the stress of the day. So if you're engaged in one of these late-night, heated conversations, my suggestion is to recognize that this argument isn't going to end your marriage, tell each other you love one another, and then go to bed holding hands. Look at your spouse and acknowledge that this discussion is not over and that you will come back to it, but that at this point, the conversation has become more destructive than constructive.

"Okay," you might say, "we know this argument isn't going to end our marriage. But, Aaron, I'm not ready to act like everything's gravy and hold her hand. That is weird and fake at this moment."

I get it. But I want you to embrace the awkwardness and hold your spouse's hand. If you can't do that, then hug for a good 30 seconds. There are a couple reasons for physical touch in this moment. First, when you end your argument and affirm the covenant of your marriage, it allows you a chance to rest and continue later from a clearer perspective. Second, physical touch helps produce oxytocin, a hormone in our body that helps us feel closer to someone or something.

You hear about oxytocin in breastfeeding and orgasm. Oxytocin is what helps the baby and mother foster that deep connection because it can come out through touch. When you hold hands through the night, or for any part of the night, you will wake up and feel better about the argument and closer to your spouse. Not only will you be rested, but now your bodies have sort of made up. You don't get to dismiss the argument, but now you are physically and emotionally closer than you were the previous night. If you want to go for a 30 second hug instead, I am fine with that as long as it is a good ole bear hug. I want full on chest to chest and not eighth grade dance style. The 30 seconds makes it difficult to be rigid for the duration of the hug, while a shorter time would allow you to be. Remember, this does not feel like the right thing to do. What our bodies *want* to do is not always what our bodies *need* to do. And in this small act, you are actively choosing your spouse even though it feels weird or fake.

The second extreme type of conflict is the couple who ignores that the conflict exists. I see this problem often. Couples using this extreme usually have one of two responses. One, they will tell you that they do not fight at all. Second, they will tell you that they do not fight very often, but when they do, it's explosive. The reason this couple will become explosive is that they've been hoarding little offenses that have become an atomic bomb. Someone may get hurt feelings repeatedly in small ways, but shut them down and continue to move forward. They don't want to rock the boat for fear of conflict and anger.

Then the other spouse will bring up something small, and that becomes the tipping point. The first spouse, who had also been hoarding offenses, feels the partner doesn't deserve to be offended. They might say, "Oh yeah, that's what's bothering you? How about I tell you the list of things you've done to offend me or upset me?" 1 Corinthians 13:5 states that love *"does not keep a record of wrongs."* At this point, the record of wrongs has been read, bombs start dropping, and both people are either ducking for cover or looking for additional ammunition. Eventually this argument will end, but the only thing to do is hope and pray that there hasn't been too much collateral damage to repair.

> "One of the healthiest investments in a marriage is healthy conflict and dialogue."

One of the healthiest investments in a marriage is healthy conflict and dialogue. The first couple who claims that they don't argue or have conflict misunderstand what I mean when I say *conflict*. Remember, the explosive way isn't a healthy model either, so when I say *conflict*, what do I mean? What is a good working definition for conflict? Dictionary.com defines *conflict* as: "to come into collision or disagreement; be contradictory, at variance, or in opposition; clash."[2]

Not every argument or conflict is an all-out brawl. If you and your spouse claim that you don't have any disagreements, either you're lying or you've long ago stopped talking. Having no disagreements *at all* is a red flag because that indicates that you no longer care. This is a scary place to be when you are no longer putting your hope and trust into your spouse. Apathy does not lead to a healthy and fulfilled marriage. You've been hurt too many times, and you're getting close to living completely separate lives, if you aren't already.

> "Apathy does not lead to a healthy and fulfilled marriage."

Love Well First: The Connection Question

Many books will discuss the best way to tackle conflict resolutions. Authors have made loads of money telling you how to talk to your spouse and how to effectively end your conflict. But an end to the conflict is only temporary. Remember, John Gottman's research states 69 percent of that conflict does not go away. It sets up camp and makes coffee every morning—because everyone needs coffee in the morning, even abstract items such as perpetual conflict. So much of the solution to healthy conflict is how we engage with our spouses prior to the conflict. Every day we have to build deposits into one another and fill each other up emotionally with love and connection in order to fight better. The reason for this is simple: when you feel connected and close to someone, you are more likely to treat one another with respect in the midst of strife. That's the hope. We still need to be careful, but if I feel disconnected from Hannah, then it's a lot easier to attack her or be critical of her. It is much easier to fight well if we love well first.

> "It is much easier to fight well if we love well first."

To help solidify this concept, ask your spouse this simple question:

How connected do you feel to me right now on a scale of one to ten?

One is barely knowing one another, just coexisting as roommates. Ten is the closest and most connected you've ever felt.

Many times, couples have individually described the status of their relationship very differently, and neither had a clue. On the connection scale, he might be at a three and she might be at an eight. This can happen at times, but it should never be a constant state.

When a couple lands on different points of the scale, one might suggest a divorce, fully expecting the other to agree and be thankful for it. However, the other spouse was completely flabbergasted, caught off guard. I've seen this happen frequently. It's devastating for couples to be so disconnected and not know it.

After you've asked how connected your spouse feels to you, follow with this basic rubric: If your spouse responds with seven or higher, you're in a pretty solid place. You may think that seven seems kind of low, but if you're at a consistent seven, you're doing well. You're not the closest you have ever felt, but you're not disconnected. The idea is to shoot for *solid* in your relationship. Shooting for nines and tens all the time is setting yourself up for failure.

If the answer is below a seven, then there is a follow up question. Ask your spouse, "What can I do this week to help move the connection in the right direction?"

If the connection is at a two, then it's unrealistic to expect to be at a seven by the end of the week, especially if you've felt disconnected for a long time. You need realistic expectations. Early on, I had many people, especially analytical people, really think long and hard about the perfect thing to move the connection. It is not designed to be rocket science. The idea is simple: communicate to your spouse what will help move the connection in the right direction. You didn't disconnect overnight, and you won't reconnect overnight, but this way you're actually headed in the right direction.

If your spouse asks you how to make the number go higher, it's your responsibility to make your answer realistic. Your answer needs to be measurable, something that both spouses can clearly state happened or did not happen. "I want to be able to trust you again" is not a tangible request. "I would love it if we could go on a date this weekend" is tangible. When you make a request, give your spouse the opportunity to make it happen and allow room for honesty.

"Absolutely let's go on a date this weekend. How's Friday night?" Or, "This week is actually extremely busy, and I don't think we can make it happen. Is there something else we could do to help our connection?" Your spouse needs to have the opportunity to say yes or no.

If you ask both of these questions on a regular basis, you should never be on completely different spectrums of the scale for too long. That's assuming you're honest. If you ask this question often and your spouse continually tells you that you are a three, you need to evaluate whether you're doing your part. If not, your connection probably won't improve, but at least then you won't be shocked. You will have willfully chosen not to reconnect with your spouse.

I try to ask my wife this question once a week. I think once a week is a good place to start. Every day is just nauseating. It may take a little while to gain traction, but if you follow through with your spouse's positive needs, then you're on your way to feeling more connected.

What do I mean by a "positive need"? A positive need is what your spouse can do for you as opposed to what you wish they were not doing. For example: "I would love it if we could spend some quality time together this evening; it would help me feel more connected to you," versus, "If you would put your phone down, then maybe we could connect this evening."

My wife calls this the rose versus thorn method. The first sentence was a positive goal. The second sentence was fighting words. It was a negative thorn focused on what the spouse wasn't doing right. You know what is going to happen? Your spouse is going to defend being on the phone or counterattack: "You're always on your phone, so why are you chewing *me* out?"

Keep the needs positive; otherwise they'll sound much more like an attack. As you begin to ask the question regularly, it's very possible to fluctuate from week to week. Hannah may feel at a seven this week and then a four next week because we have not seen each other very often. It's okay to have threes and fours. They are real and honest. We just do not want to consistently stay there. If Hannah continues to feel at a three and I do nothing to change that, then it is no wonder she would begin to resent me or be bitter with me. I have to be both aware of her needs and willing to meet them. I can't do that if I don't ask what her needs are. I want to know her well enough that I don't always need to ask. This comes back to striving for a PhD in your spouse. But we are different people, so I want to make sure that I am reading her well and meeting her needs. When we do the connection question well—asking the question and meeting the need—it makes the conflict conversations go much easier.

What did conflict look like in your childhood home? Did your parents fight all the time? Did they never fight? Some people never saw conflict in their family and grow up to be nervous about having an argument with a spouse. They thought that their parents' marriage was decent because they never saw them argue or fight. Then, when discord arrives in their marriage, they panic.

What about the person whose parents fought all the time? Many times, this person also shuts down conflict because conflict equals destruction. Neither of these examples teach children how to have healthy conflict and disagreements. No matter what conflict looked like in your childhood home, you have the potential to change the way you and your spouse have conflict discussions.

Does this mean that you need to seek counseling? Maybe. Does it mean that you are completely incompatible and should probably end your relationship? Absolutely not! *Healthy* and *conflict* are not antonyms or non sequiturs. Both mean you are normal and it's time to learn how to have these conversations in a healthy way.

CHAPTER 9

In Our Home We Forgive – Part 2

"Let us forgive each other—only then will we live in peace."
— Leo Nikolayevich Tolstoy

We are going to talk about how couples should have conflict discussions, but first there is a very important question to answer:

What are you actually fighting about?

Remember the research about 69 percent of conflict being perpetual and unsolvable? This is pretty disheartening, but also encouraging all at the same time. It's discouraging because, dang, that is a lot of conflict that can't get fixed! Sorry to you all who like to fix stuff.

But it's encouraging because every single couple has the same issue; you are not alone.

In his book *The Seven Principles for Making Marriage Work*, John Gottman discusses what he calls "dreams within the conflict."[1] His premise is simple. He says that many times, people are not really fighting about the topic they appear to be arguing about; instead, something within the conflict is causing irritation or more conflict. Couples have one or two of these dreams within the conflict that crash and fight against one another, and until we realize what they are, we will keep stepping on the same toes over and over again.

Same Issue Over and Over Again

In my marriage, it's safe to say that about 90 percent of our arguments or conflict discussions are about one area. The Bunkers have been known as a family of exaggerators, but this is not one of those occasions. And I don't think we're alone. Many couples have one or two deeper issues that continue to come up and push the other's button without even realizing it. I say "deeper issue" because I don't think most of the time we're really fighting about money, sex, punctuality, organization, parenting, or whatever may be your target of choice. "But, Aaron, we would be absolutely perfect if she would just be more willing to be intimate with me and initiate a little more. Why do I have to initiate all the time?" The real question you should ask yourself is, "What does intimacy or her pursuing you actually provide you? What deeper need is met by her pursuit of you?"

There is a reason why therapists ask about childhood so often. Our childhood affects so much of who we are as adults—what makes you think the way you do and why you respond the way you do in certain areas of your life now as an adult. Couples do themselves a disservice when they don't talk about their childhood. I don't just mean the short version of the conversation to determine whether or not each other's family are crazy. I mean continual conversations throughout your lifetime together. Many people tell me that they had terrible childhoods, but they don't want to talk about it because they've overcome it and are not continuing on the same path. I get it. But if we aren't careful, we may repeat the same habits

"Talking about our childhood helps us have self-awareness as adults."

we grew up with and not even realize it. Talking about our childhood helps us have self-awareness as adults.

The brain is such an amazing part of the body. Research on the brain is continuing to come out as we are able to discover more and more through new technology and discoveries. As a matter of fact, I saw a video recently on YouTube that showed what the brain looks like when it is happy. It was an incredible video that showed an endorphin that looked as if it were walking along the brain as smooth jazz music played in the background.[2] The brain is extremely complex, with amazing structures called synapses. Synapses are the grooves in your brain that tell your brain what to do—like a roller coaster track telling the car exactly where to go. These grooves are the reason that, when we have a conflict conversation, we already know what it's going to look like as soon as it starts. It is the reason that we have certain unreasonable fears or insecurities. Our brain is making it easy for us to keep doing repeated behaviors without having to think about it. I heard somebody say once that 80 to 90 percent of our lives are run on autopilot. I am not sure if this is scientific research but I like the picture this paints to describe your synapses. This does not mean we are checked out most of the day. It just means that we do not have to be as intentional about certain aspects of our day. I do not have to think about how to get to work, put on my clothes, or brush my teeth. I just do them because I have trained my brain to know what to do.

Do you want to hear something mind blowing? We can change our synapses! We can literally create new synapses and get rid of the old ones. Now, if we already do 80 to 90 percent on autopilot, then we have to be very intentional about changing aspects of the way our brains work. We only have 10 percent of our day that we are working with. This sounds great, but how do we change our synapses if we do not know why our brains respond the way they do in certain situations? We have to know what the synapses say in order to change them, so pay attention to what your brain's nuts and bolts look like.

> "Conflict exchange has to go deeper than the perceived issue, or the couple will keep fighting."

It's time to show you what this process can look like for a couple. Conflict exchange has to go deeper than the perceived issue, or the couple will keep fighting.

Before I jump into this story let me tell you one quick, important fact. Hannah had a freeing revelation when our kids were four weeks old, and it's stuck with me. She said, "Aaron, I have come to the conclusion that no matter how well we parent our kids, they could end up in counseling because of us." This is a sad truth but also a liberating one. Our prayer is that God helps us love and cherish our kids and also that he fills in the cracks and gaps where we struggle and miss the mark. We simply do our best, own our mistakes, work toward doing better, and trust that God is loving our kids directly by his Holy Spirit in the places where we fail. I'm telling you this because I don't want you to think that talking about our deep-rooted struggles is throwing your parents under the bus. Many parents do the best they can, but they are broken along with the rest of the world.

Consider parents who emphasize appearance, even in positive ways, such as encouraging their children to always look their best. Sometimes, parents unknowingly cause problems by a seemingly innocent action. Some women say that they've never felt attractive and that they always feel the need to lose more weight or look more like somebody else. Some of these women wonder if there is anything more to them than a body or outward appearance. Some struggle against aging because they fear losing the part of them that has been their prized asset. I'm sure the parents were trying to love their daughters well by telling them they were beautiful. But no matter how well we parent, we are still creating some of our kids' original synapses. Remember, parents are doing the best they can. I think Hannah and I would both have told you prior to getting married that we had great childhoods. And we did. We were both loved and well cared for. However, we learned once we were married that we both carried our own junk and synapses into our marriage that were deeply rooted from childhood, and they often crash into each other.

This leads us to the bathtub story.

Bathtub

Hannah loves baths. Like, for real. There are two things that I do not even have to ask Hannah if she needs: baths and massages. I mentioned earlier that we should know what makes our spouses tick in order to show them love the way they want it. Case in point, I know that Hannah always wants massages and always wants her quiet time in the bathtub. This is where she has her "thinking time." Almost every night, after the kids go down to bed, Hannah immediately prepares for her nightly thinking time. On one particular night, I passed through the bathroom to get something out of the closet and noticed that her bath water was almost to the point of overflowing. So I lovingly turned the water off. This may sound like a kind gesture, which is what I thought too, however, Hannah did not like the fact that I turned off the water. It annoyed her because she thought I was trying to control her water usage. I was offended that she didn't appreciate my helpful gesture. We started to argue, but then we paused, and Hannah and I chose to do something that has changed our conversations over conflict ever since then. We both took some time by ourselves to figure out why we were both so bothered by the other's action. This conversation seemed so silly and ridiculous, but at the same time, it also felt familiar, like there was a deeper problem beyond the tub's water level. Why have such emotions and frustrations over such a silly thing? It was silly, right? Or was it?

I went to the couch and got on my hands and knees to do some serious prayer and reflection, asking the Lord why this little incident annoyed me so much. Why was I so bothered and offended that this gesture went unnoticed, and why was I reprimanded? The answer came to me quickly: I felt as if my voice didn't matter.

For most of my life, I felt that my voice, my opinion, did not matter and therefore, I was not appreciated. I thought back through my life and the many times I felt that I was not supposed to share my opinion or my voice. Whether with my parents, other family members, church, school, or whatever. There was something deep within me that felt that my voice did not matter. This insecurity was magnified in my mind by others' reaction to me, no matter how big or small. Our reactions to our upbringing aren't always the fault of others; most of the time other people are doing their best like the rest of us. So I have this deeper issue that was not about a bathtub at all, but all of these feelings and emotions that were triggered by Hannah's scolding me for turning the water off. This may sound ridiculous, but the more I thought about this incident and the feelings associated with it, the more I realized that this was not simple at all. It was an issue that would continue to plague our marriage if I did nothing about it. I had to tackle the deeper issue.

This sounds great, but remember that couples' deeper issues often clash with one another. It sounds easy for me to just tell Hannah that I've felt for most of my life that my voice hasn't mattered, right? I really thought I would go into that bathroom after God spoke to me, share my heart with her, and move forward together. She might even apologize for triggering something within me that made me feel worthless. The problem was that it triggered something within my wife that I never intended to stir up: she felt controlled.

As Hannah sought the Lord after the tub incident, God graciously revealed why she reacted in such anger and frustration. For most of her life, she operated in fear of being controlled or manipulated. She told me that she views many areas in her life through this filter of protection from being controlled or manipulated.

So what I thought was going to be a quick "let's talk about this and move on" turned into this massive trigger for both of us. I felt as if I did not matter, and Hannah felt manipulated and controlled. Wow! I never saw that coming at all! I had no idea that Hannah thought I was trying to control her until she stated it. And Hannah was not trying to squash my voice in the process. But it happened rather quickly and subtly. From the moment those triggers were set off, we were no longer talking about the same issue. The more we talked about this issue, it became very clear to me that most of our conflicts have to do with this same issue. If we're pushing these hot buttons in one another and don't realize it, then what in the world are we supposed to do? Are we doomed in our conflict forever, or is there a way to handle these invisible time bombs?

Honor

Remember that 90 percent or more of mine and Hannah's arguments are over this one issue. Can you see why? I will give a few examples just to show you what I mean.

If I do the dishes after Hannah has said she will do them, she wonders why I'm doing them. Am I trying to manipulate her into giving me a compliment, or am I just serving her? Honestly, that is a great question and one that I constantly have to guard against. It goes back to this question: "Would we serve and love our spouses the same way we currently do if they didn't have a clue that we were doing it?" This is a great litmus test, but we can also never know the answer. It is about our motivation.

> "Would we serve and love our spouses the same way we currently do if they didn't have a clue that we were doing it?"

Hannah will obviously know I did the dishes, but why did I do them? Am I trying to show her how great I am at helping her with the chores? Or making her feel guilty for not doing them? Or am I just doing my job in loving my spouse and family well?

I've even noticed this in the way that Hannah and I have disagreements. The disagreement occurs, and Hannah will feel that I'm trying to control or manipulate her into saying what I want to hear and that she can't get it right until she walks through that magical phrase. I am trying to feel validated. I want to know that I am being heard and matter. So, when we are arguing and I do not feel validated, I want to feel heard, which in turn makes her feel manipulated and controlled. That was exhausting just typing those few sentences; you can't even imagine how tiring it is when it's occurring! Actually, you can. You and your spouse also, more than likely, have issues that butt heads with one another. You just may not know yet what that deeper area is.

Here is an example of another couple's deeper area. The husband loves to help people and needs to feel wanted and needed. He continually asks his wife how he can help her and serve her because he wants to feel needed and loved. He is the very definition of being a people pleaser. He feels validated and useful when he is helping others in need. He is an extrovert and gets energy from being around everyone and helping them in their needs. People pleasers have to be very careful about boundaries because what they may view as helping may come across differently depending on someone's circumstances. This guy loves to help others and feels alive when he does so. His ultimate joy and satisfaction come from helping his wife. He wants to love her in ways far and above others and be her knight in shining armor.

However, his wife does not like to feel that she is a bother or a nuisance, so she never asks for help and rarely accepts his help. She is an introvert and gets her energy from being by herself. It may sound silly that she would have a hard time feeling love or receiving it, but she was taught if she wanted something, she had to get it done herself. If she were to ask for things or maybe even receive them from someone else, then she was weak and a bother. She felt like a third wheel in her own family and flew under the radar. She grew up in a home that believed kids should be seen and not heard—maybe not even seen.

So what happens in this relationship? The husband will try to help his wife, and she will say she doesn't need anything at all. She is probably confused that she is being asked the question. It makes her feel awkward, and as a result she shuts it down, leading him to disconnect because now he feels that he is failing as a husband by not being able to help her.

There are other deeper issues that plague couples. Some common ones that I have seen are fear of failure, not feeling loved, fear of rejection, feelings of worthlessness, and feeling that they never measure up. This is not an exhaustive list, but I do challenge you to ask God to reveal the deeper issues in your life. Then you can have the deeper issue conversation with your spouse. You have to be in a decent place in your marriage in order to have these conversations. If Hannah and I hadn't been in a good place relationally when the bathtub conversation occurred, I might have said something like, "I am not someone from your past who has controlled or manipulated you, so don't treat me like I am." Hannah might have said something like, "Don't be so sensitive," or, "That is ridiculous. Of course you matter. Just don't control me."

If we can't have the deeper conversation about the deep issues, then we can't share what it triggered in the other person. The fact is that every issue, even ones in an individual, no matter where it originated, is a marriage issue. I'm not saying that you're both equally at fault. That is something different. But it is a marriage issue, not just a his or her issue, because we're called to *"carry one another's burdens"* (Gal. 6:2). You may not be able to work with your spouse right now, but you can work on yourself. I do encourage you to work toward being able to share the information with your spouse, but if you can't have the conversation with them right now, please talk to a trusted friend, advisor, or counselor to help you ask some deep questions about the way your brain works. All you can change in marriage is you.

Now that you have some idea of what these deeper issues are, what do you do with them? This is a very simple concept, but not very easy to execute.

Honor the other person. I have to honor the fact that Hannah uses a filter rooted in manipulation and control and recognize that in her. I cannot negate her issues. I have to be careful and not manipulate or control her, and I must assure her that my heart is not to hurt her. And Hannah has to honor my fear that I don't matter and show that she cares about me. She assures me that I matter and that my voice and opinion matter and that she loves me.

Most couples don't hurt each other on purpose. I've asked many people how often they wake up and just want to punch their spouses in the face. Do they really want to deliver a Rocky Balboa uppercut to their jaw? How often do they want to just go at it? Maybe they expect to fight, but most don't *want* to fight.

How often do you feel that your spouse wants to go at it? Do they want to go for the jugular the moment that your head rises from the pillow? The results are very different. Nobody has ever stated that they wanted to fight, maybe every now and then, but not normally. But many times, people think their spouses want to fight. This tells me that neither spouse wants to fight but that they both may be expecting a fight. This is like walking into the situation with your dukes up. You already have your fists up, ready for the fight, even though you don't plan on throwing a punch. Your spouse says something simple or neutral, and you take it as offense and jab back. You aren't trying to bring up deeper, painful issues in your spouse, but you may very well be doing just that. When that happens, own it and lead with an apology.

I think most arguments start over one of two things — hurt feelings and misunderstandings. There may be plenty of times in an argument when you feel innocent and may have a hard time apologizing.

There are two extreme types of apologies. The first is the flippant apology. Your spouse tells you that what you just said or did devastated them and you quickly reply, "I'm so sorry; it won't happen again. Now, what is for dinner?" Okay, maybe you're not that quick to ask for dinner. Maybe you wait 10 minutes or so to ask. But if this happened, I would think that you didn't understand the word "devastation." This person probably does not want to fight and just wants to apologize in order to keep peace and keep the gravy train rolling.

The second extreme apology is the one that will not come until the offender fully understands what they are apologizing for. This person asks so many questions that the offended person may feel interrogated. The person who uses this apology tactic is trying to justify their actions. The problem is that you may never get it. It's a miracle when we completely get it because we are so different, our brains work differently, and our synapses are triggered differently.

In any situation, there are always two perspectives of reality, and they are both real. I cannot change the way Hannah perceived a situation or something I said, and she cannot change my perception. Take a church sermon for example. If you have a conversation with your spouse afterward, you may have very different ideas about what the take-away points were and what the sermon was about. That is why we cannot tell each other how to feel or apologize for how the other person felt. We can only apologize for our part. Because we have two different realities of the same event or occurrence, it would make little sense to argue about what happened.

If we argue, it will go something like this: "We are fighting because you are not showing affection, and I am feeling taken advantage of." Then the other spouse counters, "We are fighting because you came in with a bad attitude and were mean and then somehow want me to just be all lovey-dovey." This conversation will not go anywhere. The only way to have these conversations is to talk about our own perceptions and how we feel. (I know. There we go talking about feelings again.) We talk about our feelings because we don't want to fight over misunderstandings.

Talking through our feelings helps to keep us from comparing ourselves and living in judgment. We are not called to live in comparison or judgment. We are called to live like Christ. If I justify why my sin is not as bad as Hannah's, then I have to look in the mirror and get the massive log of hypocrisy out of my own face (Matt. 7:1–5). We do it because we want to feel better about ourselves, but we don't get our purpose and joy from comparing ourselves to others. We get our joy and hope in the Lord and in him alone.

Even in your conflict, treat your spouse with respect. There have been many times in conflict that looking back on the situation I realized that I was acting like my three-year-olds. I wanted my way, and when I didn't get it, I pouted or became disrespectful. We have to be better than three-year-olds, or what kind of example are we for them? I can't tell them a certain behavior or response is inappropriate and then act the same way when I don't get my way.

When you try to resolve a conflict, take turns talking about how you feel and then validate each other where you are. When having a conversation about conflict management, make sure you are both in a place physically and mentally to have the conversation. It won't solve conflict if you're both heated and seeing red. Breathe and come back to the situation. Just don't wait too long. We want to keep small things small and not build resentment. The goal of this conversation is now

> "The goal of this conversation is now understanding, not agreeing or even justifying."

understanding, not agreeing or even justifying. The best way is to take turns. One person begins, and rather than focusing on discussing the actions of the other person, they state how they felt about a situation using "I felt" statements. They say things like, "I felt sad," or "I felt angered," or "I felt rejected." The other person is trying to understand where the spouse is coming from. Remember, you may never completely get it, but seek to understand and then validate your spouse.

Many people don't know what I mean when I say "validate a feeling or an emotion." I do not mean just saying the words, "I validate you." I've heard someone say that in response to his spouse, and it comes across as apathetic. It's more than that. It's trying to jump into the other person's head to ask the right questions so that you can say, "Based on what you're saying and your perception, I can see why you feel that way," and mean it. That does not mean you agree. I'm asking you to empathize.

There are many times when couples offend each other by accident. A husband compliments his wife on her shoes, and she gets upset and tells him he's rude and insensitive. They could argue forever that he was or wasn't being rude. The husband can't change or control how his wife is feeling. She is feeling hurt and angered. He may not understand it, but it is her reality. She is experiencing that feeling, and her feelings are valid. However, feelings also lie. Feelings can mislead you. If they have time, the husband can ask deeper questions about the significance of this pain and why she had that reaction. Either way, he still owes his wife an apology.

"What? He was innocent, Aaron! He gave her a compliment, and she went berserk!"

True. But, he still has to own his part. He hurt her, whether or not it was on purpose. He has to own the fact that he hurt her before she cares that it was not on purpose. He should say, "I am sorry I hurt you. That was not my intention." Notice he doesn't say, "I am sorry *you* are hurt." He cannot apologize for how *she* feels; he can only apologize for his part. Lead with an apology. I am not advocating a woe-is-me attitude in which you always feel that you are in the wrong. I am saying that "they don't care how much you know, until they know how much you care." We could, if we wanted to, apologize every day to our kids and our spouses because every day we *"fall short of the glory of God"* (Rom. 3:23). Every. Day. The more you own your hurt and apologize for causing pain, the more your spouse begins to believe you over time.

I once heard in a conference that we should ask ourselves if we think our spouses are out to get us. If the answer is no, then maybe we should try to give them the benefit of the doubt. However, if trust has been broken and hearts have been inappropriately handled, it takes time to restore the relationship. Restoration starts with "I'm sorry." Forgiveness is a one-way street, but reconciliation takes two, as the saying goes. When we are wronged, we look for a debt to be paid—perhaps an apology. When we choose to forgive someone, we aren't canceling the debt; we're just no longer responsible for collecting the debt. We're letting God collect the debt owed. You are able to forgive more easily when you keep in perspective the amount that God has forgiven you for. Forgiveness is a process; it's not always a one-time decision. I cannot control whether or not my wife forgives me for my erroneous ways and bad habits. All I can do is to ask for her forgiveness and try to look more like Christ tomorrow.

> "Forgiveness is a process; it's not always a one-time decision."

Colossians 3:19 states, *"Husbands, love your wives and don't be bitter toward them."* Hannah will hurt me, just as I will hurt her. But we both have a mandate to not be resentful toward one another. Offenses will come (Luke 17:1), but I have a choice of forgiveness or bitterness toward her, and I should choose to focus on loving her more.

A friend recently had a realization about forgiveness and owning his own part. He told me that his wife was getting irritated and frustrated at him for something he didn't even know he was doing wrong. He said that in the past, he would have become defensive and maybe even offered a counterattack to help protect himself. However, this time he realized the fact that his wife was feeling triggered, so he chose to love her well, and focus on his part, instead of controlling her or attacking her. He realized that when he fought back to defend himself, he and his wife would argue, both hurt and defensive. However, when he responded well and loved her through it, she was able to think about her actions and responses. Later she came back to him and said that he'd done nothing wrong; she was being triggered because of how she was treated as a young girl.

When we focus on our part and love and forgive our spouses well, our spouses are able to look inward at their own brokenness and wrongdoing. It's almost as if our brains have a hard time comprehending why someone loves us and forgives us when we aren't treating them in kindness and love. We can't comprehend it, and we're forced to look deeper inside ourselves. Forgiveness can lead to a change in others' responses and behaviors.

CHAPTER 10

In Our Home We Have Purpose

"The person without a purpose is like a ship without a rudder."

—Thomas Carlyle

What do you do?

It's the dreaded question that everybody asks early on in a conversation with the goal of creating small talk and learning more about one another. I hate that question, and so does my wife. Even as I typed it, I saw her face making that twist that indicates how annoyed she is at the question. We hate that question because what you do does not define you or who you are. What are you supposed to say if you are a homemaker or if you're just getting started in your business venture? You love what you do, but you feel that you have to defend your career choice. You know what you want to say: "I'm a homemaker and love what I do." This may be absolutely true, but you feel you have to give a long, elaborate answer with quantifiers so people don't think differently of you.

One of the main reasons I did not go to my high school reunion was that I felt I had nothing to show for the 10 years I had been out. I was married, but I had no children. I had a job I wasn't ecstatic about, and we were barely making ends meet. I felt I had nothing to offer. How sad is that? I based whether or not to go to a reunion on what I had to show people. I wanted to be able to brag and show people what accomplishments I had, and when I searched in my Mary Poppins bag of tricks, I came up with a big wad of nothing. So I did not go.

The truth is too many people find their identity and purpose in things or circumstances that quickly fade. Rick Warren wrote a whole book, *The Purpose Driven Life*[1] —a *New York Times* Best Seller—because we are all so desperately searching for purpose. Why are we here? If you struggle with this answer, you may be looking for your identity in things of this world and not living to your full purpose.

Am I Supposed to Provide?

The idea of provision and the pressure that some put on their shoulders to provide, especially men, can feel insurmountable. It's a high stress drive that motivates men, and it's very easy to get identity and self-esteem from how much or how little is in our bank accounts. In December 2013, I had an experience that caused me to rethink everything I had ever thought about provision and my role in it.

As I mentioned earlier, when Hannah and I got married, I worked at the coffee capital empire, Starbucks. I worked there for several years prior to getting married, and soon after, I realized that I needed to make a little more money to support us. I was married now, and I told myself I had to step it up—Starbucks wasn't going to cut it much longer. At this point, I had not started grad school and had no idea when that venture would begin. I had always been good with numbers, and I loved people and interacting with them, so I thought that being in banking made sense. I applied and got a job working as a teller for a large bank. I started out as a part-time teller and continued to work part-time at Starbucks. After six months, I was promoted to full-time teller. At this point I finally decided to quit working at Starbucks and work full-time at the bank.

I loved being a teller. I enjoyed handling money, and I thrived on my everyday interactions with bank customers. Prior to working in the banking industry, I didn't realize that there were "regulars" in the banking world, but there are. I learned people's stories, and it felt wonderful being able to help people with their banking transactions while showing and expressing love as a teller. I knew early on that I did not want to be a banker because there was too much pressure in sales. I love people, but I do not love trying to sell people stuff. I would rather just sit with them and have a long conversation about the deeper issues of their hearts. However, after one year of teller experience, they offered me a position as a banker. Even though I knew I would not enjoy it, I took it because I had been married a couple of years and needed to make more money. I wanted to look good for my wife and help her be proud of me. After all, it is a man's job to provide, right? Or is it?

When we're trying to please others above all else and finding our identity in places, or money, or positions of authority, we will never feel satisfied. I made a crucial error in accepting the position, and I knew it the day I accepted the offer. I made up my mind that the raise was worth losing my happiness and joy, but when they presented me the dollar amount, it wasn't even close to what I'd been told it would be. It was barely larger than I was making as a teller, yet I did it anyway because it was a raise. I convinced myself that the calling on my life to help change marriages wasn't really in my cards. Maybe I was supposed to be a banker and make money and help provide the American Dream to my bride and our future family.

Whenever you substitute God's calling on your life for what you want to do, it will never give you what you thought it was going to. It will always come up short. Look at anyone in Scripture who thought he or she had a better plan than God's. Adam and Eve ate the forbidden fruit. Abraham slept with his wife's maidservant. The people of Egypt wandered around in the desert for 40 years. Saul ignored a command. David slept with a married woman. The Bible is full of examples of people who thought they knew better than God. God allowed them to pursue their own desires because he is gracious and a gentleman and he does not force us into

> "Whenever you substitute God's calling on your life for what you want to do, it will never give you what you thought it was going to."

anything. If you hear clearly from God on an issue, it will save you a lot of pain and heartache to head that direction now instead of choosing another route. If you are currently running from what God has spoken to you, turn it around. There is still hope. Get back on the path. God spoke clearly to me while I was in Colorado, telling me that I was meant to help marriages, bring them back to life, and guide them to look and sound as he had designed them in the first place.

But here I was, three years later, questioning my identity and forgetting my calling in pursuit of monetary gains. I had a large weight on my shoulders to provide and felt that I had to do everything I could do to make that happen. I knew God was my provider, but I didn't live like it. I knew it in my mind, but didn't believe it in my heart. I lived as if all the pressure was on me, and as a result I was miserable. I was living in a prison made by my own pressures and demands.

I was a decent banker, but I hated going to work, even though I loved the customers and enjoyed most of my coworkers (there is always that one). I woke up every morning waiting for the day to be over and dreading the next 8 to 12 hours. I had been working for a long time and never felt that way even about the most mundane jobs I'd had. I started and finished grad school while working as a banker. God is so gracious and loving to us even though we make it harder on ourselves. He never ditches us; he will never leave you nor forsake you (Deut. 31:6).

At the beginning of the book of Exodus, the Israelites were still in captivity and had been for 400 years. Before their miraculous delivery, they were slaves. Even in the midst of their slavery, the Israelites prayed to God. I know this because Exodus 2:24 states, *"So God heard their groaning and He remembered."* I am thankful that God hears us and remembers.

Hannah and I had been praying for a change and asking for God's favor but did not know where to go. After I finished my master's degree, I was too afraid to make a big change like quitting my job and looking for a full-time counseling job while I finished up my state licensure for counseling. I didn't know where to go or what to do. During this time, we were still faithful in our prayers and our commitment to one another. Hannah was so kind and gracious to me during these difficult years. We were progressing in our marriage, but we were having difficulty getting pregnant. We had always felt the call to adopt, and during these difficult work years, we entered into the plan of adoption.

I was working a job I couldn't stand and Hannah was working for a dear friend of ours. We had turned in all of our paperwork to our adoption agency, had just received our preapproval letter, and were scheduled for our homestudy to begin within the month to be officially approved and added to the list of waiting parents. I was going to continue working at the bank while I became a fully licensed counselor with the state of Texas. We had all our ducks lining up after years of struggle to start a family. But, in December 2013, God answered our prayer in a dramatic moment that I never saw coming.

My typical schedule was to work Monday at the bank, then Tuesday at a counseling center, then back at the bank Wednesday through Saturday, and back at the counseling center on Sunday. I was working every day of the week with no time for rest or recharging. On the second Wednesday in December 2013, it happened. My life changed in a matter of hours. When you pray, you never really know when a breakthrough or an answer is going to come or what it is going to look like. I have realized many times in my own life that answers to prayers don't look anything like what I had imagined.

On that memorable Wednesday, God lovingly but swiftly pushed me out of the nest. I was fired from the bank. I never saw it coming. My integrity, honesty, and reputation had come under an onslaught. I highly valued and prided myself on my integrity, and then it was all taken away in something I did not realize at the time I was doing wrong.

I took the walk of shame to my car and was not allowed to say goodbye to any of my coworkers. It was humiliating and embarrassing and very confusing. I called Hannah as soon as I was in the car and told her the hardest thing I have ever had to tell her. "I . . . I was . . . fired." The normally 15-minute drive home took me 45 minutes, partially because of the traffic, but also because I was sobbing. I had no idea how to breathe. I had to remind myself that it was going to be okay.

I had a decision to make then: was I going to trust God with all I had and pursue full-time counseling, or go find another banking job? I decided that night that even though I did not get out of the nest willingly, I was not going to get back in. I would learn how to fly and that meant pursuing full-time counseling as an intern counselor with the state of Texas. I had lost my purpose working at the bank. I had lost my

> "I was trying to do God's role myself and not allowing him to do his part."

identity because I was no longer the provider. I was failing my wife and our future children because we had already started the process of adoption. I felt like I was failing at being a dad before I even officially had the title.

Two days later, as I was searching for jobs and picking up the pieces of my shattered ego, God spoke to me clearly. I like to be real with God. He knows what's in my heart, so I might as well not hold it back in my prayers. It was during an honest moment like this that God told me, "Aaron, you are not the provider for your family. I am." It was so overwhelmingly beautiful and powerful to me to know that I do not have to carry the weight of being a provider. Even as I typed those words, tears filled my eyes because God is so good. I had placed my identity and purpose into something that was not even part of my role; no wonder it was such a heavy burden. I was trying to do God's role myself and not allowing him to do his part. I quickly found scriptures to help solidify the words in my heart. In Matthew 6 and Luke 12 (it's the same story, just in two different places) Jesus talks about this pressure. In my Bible, the heading for both of these sections is *The Cure for Anxiety*. I hadn't even realized my anxiety because of the pressure I had put on myself to provide. Jesus knows you need food and clothes. He says *"Don't keep striving for what you should eat and what you should drink, and don't be anxious. For the Gentile world eagerly seeks all*

> "I cannot put my purpose or identity in other things. I have to put my identity in Christ and in him alone."

these things, and your Father knows that you need them. But seek His kingdom, and these things will be provided for you"

(Luke 12:29–31). The pressure is not on me. My role is to trust God and seek his kingdom above everything else, and he will take care of me.

I cannot put my purpose or identity in other things. I have to put my identity in Christ and in him alone.

A few days later, we got a phone call telling us that there was a mom who had just given birth to twins, and the agency was considering us as adoptive parents. We were so excited, yet freaked out at the same time. We'd been waiting for our children for so long, and now here they were, but their potential dad didn't have a job. We were dreading telling our agency about my job situation, thinking that we were no longer *worthy* of parenthood and that they would kick us to the curb. But God orchestrated the conversation with our social worker so well that it was nothing I needed to stress over. I told her that I no longer worked at the bank but was hoping to make close to the same amount of money doing full-time counseling. Our social worker thought nothing of it and simply said, "Great!" and then gave us the details of the kids. They were boy and girl twins who had been born a week earlier. They were in the NICU for a few days and then in foster care briefly before we brought them home on December 30, 2013.

God's plans are always better than ours. He works in the details so intricately and doesn't miss anything. He knew I couldn't be working at the bank with all the stress while at the same time being a new father to twins. When God closes a door, he almost always opens another one. Monday, December 9, was my last full day of work at the bank. God did not miss a single step. The moment when I thought my life was falling apart, God was orchestrating the next chapter we'd been waiting on for many years. The faulty ground that I had placed my purpose in had to be torn down in order for another to grow, and God knew the timing for it all. Do you know when my kids were born? December 9—the same day one door closed, a much greater door opened wide!

It's Not All about the Job

I already hear some of you saying that the job situation doesn't apply to you and that you are not running from a call on your life. Praise God! Our job is not the only place that we can find our identity or our calling. The question boils down to this: are you living as God has called you to live? Are you living out your full *imago Dei*? Our what? *Imago Dei*. Genesis 1:27 states that we were created in the *imago Dei*. Translated, this means the "image of God." Even though we all look and act different, we are all created in that same image of God. The purpose of our lives should be to love God with all of our hearts and then love people. This idea that God made us in his image means that we all have attributes of God in us, but how we love God and people with all of our hearts may look and sound very different. He made you unique. Embrace who God has called *you* to be. Your identity is a son or daughter of God. Your identity is not anyone's job but yours. You get your identity from your relationship with your Creator. I want you to embrace all of you, to find your identity in Christ, and be who he uniquely created you to be.

Nobody on the planet looks and sounds exactly like you. Some people talk about having a doppelganger, someone who looks a lot like you. My doppelganger is an old baby. I have a head that has a few hairs on it (God knows how many hairs are on your head too, even if it is not easy to count like mine is) and skin so soft that my fingers bleed peeling hardboiled eggshells. Actors have body doubles, and you may have a doppelganger, but there is no other you. You are special and one of a kind. Don't forget how special and unique you are, no matter what others have told you and no matter what others have claimed over your life, even if your spouse doesn't give you the love and attention that you crave. These strong words, although they hurt immensely, do not define who you are. You are so much more than your weaknesses and shortcomings.

Who Are You?

The Bible says that we are all important. 1 Corinthians 12:12–26 compares the body of Christ to a literal body. It states that all parts of the body are important. The foot has to operate as a foot and not a mouth—although there have been many times when I've stuck my foot in my mouth. The hands can't get jealous of the legs, because they all have an important role to play. Each has a specific function and role. Can you imagine a body with all hands? Hands everywhere? It would be the 11th plague from Exodus—the plague of too many hands to count. It sounds like something out of Greek mythology or DC Comics. Just like you need your hands and your feet to act as hands and feet, we need to act out our roles.

Who are you? What defines you? What makes you special and unique? These are questions you need to know the answer to. Many times it takes our spouses to help us see through our own junk and tell us who we are in Christ. According to research from the US Department of Health and Human Services, PBS, and the National Association of Anorexia Nervosa and Associated Disorders in February 2017, about 91 percent of women struggle with body image.[2] When 91 percent of women look into a mirror, what do they see? Do they see their perfect curves and something that they are proud of? No, they see their imperfections or the things they feel that they need to improve. They see the junk. Most men are able to tell their wives how ridiculous that is and tell them how beautiful they are. This does not necessarily mean that the lady automatically agrees with him and changes her view of herself. However, it does mean that she doesn't have somebody who validates her brokenness and insecurities.

We all have those insecurities and struggles. If someone close to us were to point them out, it would sting. Many of us see our blemishes when we look into the mirror of our lives. We see the lack. We see the areas that are not quite where we want them to be. We see a broken shell of what we wish we were. If our spouses or those close to us tell us how much we lack, it becomes real. The woman whose husband agrees that she has blemishes is speaking death over his spouse. Remember we have to speak life!

Vision

Our job as spouses is to pull out God in one another. Larry Crabb wrote a book called *Soul Talk*.[3] The general idea of this book asks, "What if we took our everyday conversations and chitchat and took those as opportunities to pull out Christ in one another?" One of the reasons we don't have the deeper conversations about what moves our souls is that we feel many don't care to hear it. There is a saying that my friends say about me: "Aaron goes deeper, faster." I want to dig deep and pull out the real. I want to have hard conversations, and I want to be able to pull out each of their *imago Dei*. I can't pull out their *imago Dei* if all I ever see is their mask. I need to see them in their raw, vulnerable states in order to help pull out Christ in them.

In Larry Crabb's book, he has a chapter called "Think Vision." The purpose of this chapter is to think what the other's vision is during your conversations with them. To see what they're really talking about. What are their real struggles and issues? What is the vision that God has for them? In the video series that goes with the book, he shares a vision letter that he wrote to his spouse. The purpose of the letter was to show the audience and readers what it looks like to pull Christ out in one another. I absolutely loved the idea and have stolen it and use it every year. Hannah and I write vision letters to one another every Valentine's Day. This is our gift to one another rather than a box of chocolates and a few carnations. We want to intentionally pull out Christ in one another. Of course we want to do this all the time, but at least once a year we take time to intentionally put it on paper so that the other person has a tangible vision to hold on to. The letter is written with this premise: What would your life look like if you lived completely abandoned to Christ? If there was nothing holding you back, if you were able to step outside your struggles and fears and live completely for God, what would it look like?

I have realized that for those who are not used to pulling out Christ in one another, this can be a daunting task, so I'm going to provide an example of a vision letter.

Keep in mind, your vision and your purpose will look different from this one. You should adapt it to fit your spouse. My wife has graciously allowed me to include the vision letter that I wrote to her for Valentine's Day in 2016.

Vision Letter

Hannah, you are an amazing example of Godly beauty and love. You have come so far in your walk with the Lord this past year, and it has been encouraging and inspiring to watch you grow. You have experienced motherhood with grace, and even through trials and tribulations you have remained steadfast and strong.

My vision is for you to continue to walk in what God has called you to do. He has called you to create and to not stop creating. At times you get caught up on the details and the semantics and let your brain talk you out of certain things. My prayer is for a free mind and clarity of purpose. I want you to be uninhibited in your pursuit of God this coming year. Your health does not need to be a sore in your side but may be a platform to talk about the goodness, mercy, and healing power of Jesus Christ. Though you may fall, he will not slay you. I am so proud of your strength and your courage, but at times I think you let that strong exterior prevent you from being vulnerable and raw with the Lord and your family. My prayer is that you continue to trust the vulnerability process and the unveiling of your heart. You are strong and you are courageous but that does not mean you don't get hurt or that you can't bleed. When you feel sad and hurt and discouraged, that does not mean that you don't trust God.

You are an amazing mother, and every day I am thankful that the kids get to experience the joy and laughter you bring. You are an intentional mother who does not let the routine hold you back. Continue to pursue your kids and continue to pursue your giftings. Continue to pursue God, because when you do that, you are unstoppable. God loves to see you dance and sing and laugh. He delights in knowing you and your heart.

Your voice changes people. Your presence brings a peace and a calm to a room. Embrace the calming and peaceful presence that you carry. You are a peacemaker, but don't confuse that with peacekeeping. Don't be afraid to walk into a situation that may seem hairy or daunting, because you carry peace with you and God wants you to make peace in the midst of the chaos and the storm. Don't avoid the storms or the noise, but instead head straight into the storm and create peace in it!

My vision for you this coming year is MORE! More creativity! More freedom! More liberty! More passion! More love! More Jesus! More, More, More! Don't be afraid for the more of your life; just get ready for it!

So, start thinking about the purpose that God has called you and your spouse to and start acting it out.

CHAPTER 11

In Our Home We Are Real

"She warned him not to be deceived by appearances, for beauty is found within."
—Beauty and the Beast

This rule may sound silly and weird at first glance, but it's one of the most important rules for our family and one that cannot be ignored or taken lightly. What does being real mean? Aren't we all real people? Yes, but we are not always being real. Let me explain. A relationship will only move forward and grow in depth to the level that you're vulnerable. When I say that we are real, I mean that we are raw, vulnerable, and exposed. My definition of being vulnerable is "the potential to be hurt." I put myself out there, with vulnerability, knowing that it may not go well and I may regret my move.

Here is a simple example of being vulnerable in a marriage. Hannah might say, "I feel like I was a bad mom today." She is expressing a raw piece of her heart that is fragile and delicate. The way I handle these words is very important. I could ask her, "Why do you feel like a bad mom today? Were you on your phone all day again?" I could say that. And if I am honest, in my flesh at times I may be thinking that; but should I really say that? You may laugh at that question, but you may be surprised at the number of people who think that response is an appropriate and valid question. Notice that Hannah did not ask me if she should feel like a bad mom, nor did she ask me to tell her how she messed it up and validate her negative feelings. What she did took guts and courage because she expressed a perceived brokenness in herself or a crack in her armor. She was already feeling like a bad mom and did not need me to tell her that it was true. In my hypothetical response, I indicated that she could not trust me with her vulnerabilities; and I guarantee you that the next day, she will not tell me that she feels like a bad mom. I took an opportunity to grow in intimacy and connection and in essence told her to hold in her insecurities and vulnerabilities because I was not a safe place for the words to land.

> "A relationship will only move forward and grow in depth to the level that you're vulnerable."

Vulnerability

Let's rewind to early spring 2006. I was about to go on my first date with Hannah at the infamous Pei Wei. It was the night of the big event that would change my life forever, but I felt God tell me something that night prior to the date that frightened me, although I knew it to be true. If you remember back to the beginning of the book, I told you I had always liked girls, but they rarely liked me back. There was one girl before Hannah whom I really liked. In fact, I actually thought I loved her. I won't go into the details of that whole story, but I will tell you this: it did not go well. It went horribly the entire time. I felt that I had put my heart on the line and had come up empty and broken. I was afraid and didn't want to ever feel that pain again.

Then Hannah came into my life. She was special, and I was so excited about our date that I almost couldn't stand it. I was also really nervous. After I got ready for the date, I sat at the edge of my bed and prayed. I prayed for God to have his way in this date and for me to be able to lead with grace and humility as an example of him on our date. As I sat there praying, I felt God tell me that the only way for this relationship to possibly work was if I was willing to put my heart completely on the line again.

Was I willing to have my heart broken all over again? Did I trust God with my heart? I loved God, but I didn't want to put my heart on the line again. I cannot tell you how scary that request felt, but also how liberating it was because I could not control the situation. I had to leave it up to God. I sat there that evening and told God that I would trust him completely; I would be willing to have my heart broken all over again if he wanted me to put it on the line.

Remember I told you that I told her everything about my life and all of my baggage on the first night? This required putting my heart on the chopping block. I'm not sure that's what God meant when he asked me to be willing to have my heart broken again, but I didn't waste any time with that request.

God was teaching me early on that vulnerability was the only way our relationship ever had a chance. One night we were on the phone while I was still in Colorado, and I told Hannah how much protecting her heart meant to me. I told her that I wanted to honor her heart and cherish her so that even if I wasn't the person she was going to marry, her heart would suffer no damage. It's a privilege to have the heart or even a piece of the heart of another human being, even in dating and engagement. Do not take that privilege for granted. Your potential spouse-to-be is putting a lot on the line and giving you enormous potential for good or bad. Remember the famous line from *Spider-Man?* Uncle Ben tells him, "With great power comes great responsibility." Any person who has had the honor of being loved by someone has great power, and they have a responsibility to cherish that heart and take great care of it. I wanted to honor Hannah's heart for her future husband, even if that guy wasn't me. I wanted to honor her and let her be real.

In marriage, you have to choose to give your heart to the other person every single day. Hannah has my heart. She does not have my everything because I love God first, then Hannah. But she has me. I am so in love with that redhead. I choose to give my heart to her every day. It's not a one-time decision. When you're in a healthy, life-giving relationship, it becomes easy to give your heart away every day; but I still get to choose to give it to her. I want to handle her heart with care. Visualize a beating heart in your hand. A human heart would fit in the palm of an average adult's hand. I try to picture her heart beating in my hand, and I have to handle it with care. If I move too quickly, I may drop it or puncture it. If I'm too careless or too concerned with myself and forget that I have her heart, I can quickly damage it. If she is going to be vulnerable and put her heart in my hand, then I have to take good care of it.

> "In marriage, you have to choose to give your heart to the other person every single day."

Safe Place

What does it mean to be a safe place? Think of a cloud, a heavenly little cloud that the vulnerability just floats to and rests on. The vulnerability is resting on the cloud. That is the picture I want you to remember when you think of being a safe place. I have a place on my chest where Hannah rests her head that she calls "my nook." It is her nook, and she alone has it. She feels safe there and at peace. In order for people to be vulnerable in marriage or relationships, they have to know that it is safe for them to do so. They need to feel that it is emotionally safe to express themselves.

There are plenty of people in my life I choose not to be vulnerable with because it does not feel like a safe environment to do so. If I express raw and sensitive information to someone who doesn't handle it well, then it is unlikely I'll continue to be vulnerable. I choose to lead with vulnerability because that is a culture that I want to cultivate among people. I want to live in a world where we are all vulnerable and real rather than living behind our masks of discomfort or shame. If I continue to be vulnerable to others who continue to shut me down, then I shouldn't be surprised when I'm hurt. I have to learn how to protect myself and my family. I once heard a phrase from Steven Furtick (pastor of Elevation Church in North Carolina) that I really enjoyed. He said that he doesn't burn down bridges, but that he does put weight limits on the bridges. I'm not going to shun people and forever kick them out of my life, but if they continue to not be a safe place, then I am no longer going to put as much weight on what they say or what they don't say. When we put boundaries up with others, we teach them that we matter and that we have to protect ourselves. Boundaries are not a negative thing; they're a must!

If you're not used to being vulnerable, learn to be balanced in how much you share. Don't tell your spouse that you need to be vulnerable and then say, "I've been miserable in our marriage for the last 40 years." That is not the place to start. Start with small things, such as sharing that you feel frustrated with your performance at work. The best place to start with vulnerability is to start outside your marriage. It's a lot easier to be vulnerable with areas that have nothing to do with your spouse than it will be for you to be vulnerable about your marriage. You can be vulnerable about your childhood or something that's easier and more comfortable to talk about.

One thing I have experienced is that sometimes people know when they are being vulnerable, but they may not know when their spouses are being vulnerable. As you're learning vulnerability, it's a great idea to let your spouse know when you are being vulnerable. When you start the conversation letting your spouse know you're being vulnerable, you're letting them assume a new role in the conversation, as opposed to being a spectator, because your heart is about to be exposed and raw. Your spouse immediately readies to receive your words with tender care and grace.

Now, I'm not trying to state that every vulnerable conversation will be difficult or tough to hear, but the listener still has a major role to play. When Hannah tells me she's had a hard day and feels like a bad mom, I have to be a safe place. I may tell her something like, "I'm sorry you had a rough day. You probably did a great feat in just surviving today. It's okay; some days are as tough as nails to deal with." The words aren't as important as the feeling and the atmosphere in the room. Do you judge her, or do you allow her to be real and exposed and loved through the process? Are you safe? Does she feel safe expressing her deepest desires and fears to you?

Hannah and I have been practicing vulnerability for a long time, but there are still times in our marriage that I will tell her when I'm about to be vulnerable. We still at times tell each other when we we're being vulnerable. There is no shame in telling someone your vulnerability. As a matter of fact, telling someone is being brave and vulnerable—a great place to start.

It's Not Always Funny

My kids are hilarious, and they laugh a lot. Anytime I'm feeling down, I can just hang around my kids and they'll inevitably laugh at something I've said. They say, "That's funny, Daddy," and at the moment, nothing else matters. Even if my jokes are corny, they still laugh with me or at me. Their genuine giggles and joy give me the feels all over.

I love to laugh, but there are times when we're not supposed to laugh. Some moments call for seriousness or delicacy. If I were to tell Hannah a vulnerable issue and she laughed at me, I would feel embarrassed and ashamed. I would also feel as if something were wrong with me. However, if I tell Hannah that I'm being vulnerable and then proceed to tell her about my insecurities while I am giggling or smiling, then she may be very confused.

Inappropriate affect. That is what happens if I am laughing at my vulnerable moment. This happens all the time with couples. Basically, the facial expressions or reactions don't match the words spoken. For example, a woman may tell you that she doesn't feel beautiful but then follows it up with a joke about why people don't find her attractive. This usually happens because somewhere in childhood or early adulthood, she learned that her emotions don't matter. It's easier to laugh than cry. The little boy who fell running to first base learned that he can laugh at his pain because crying doesn't solve anything.

I get it. I get why someone would rather laugh through pain than cry about it. The problem, however, is that your spouse may not know you're being vulnerable if your face or attitude shows something completely different. Your spouse is confused when you laugh at something that is not funny, and the brain has a hard time processing that. Most of the time, especially if your spouse isn't aware of what's happening, they will laugh with you.

Someone who struggles with using an inappropriate response such as defaulting to humor probably laughs a lot and has a lot of fun but may struggle having "deeper" conversations or even really knowing what that means. There are also those who don't show any emotion and come off as robotic. People with inappropriate response may avoid conflict out of fear. They may use humor as deflection or self-preservation. Any conversation that is not neutral or happy will be difficult for them, and they will gracefully bow out.

People who struggle with inappropriate responses have to learn several things. First, they have to learn how to have vulnerable conversations without fear of reproach. They also have to learn how to sit with their spouses when they are being vulnerable. At times, I have couples who both struggle with using humor. This couple has so much fun! They do a lot together and have a great time when things are going well. When they're not having fun, they're usually at odds because one person may attempt vulnerability, but the other is thrown off and attempts to bring back the happy laughing train. They are deathly afraid of being hurt or found weak.

I heard a story one time of an eight-year-old boy who was taken from his family out of neglect from his parents. He was the eldest of several kids, and as the eldest, he felt a responsibility for his younger siblings. This pressure was exacerbated when the police officer who was trying to help told him that he had to be strong for his siblings because his siblings needed him—he couldn't show weakness. I understand what the police officer was trying to do; he was trying to help the young man cope and be strong in the midst of tough times. Here is the problem with that: it was a tough time, and the young boy felt that he could no longer show that he was hurting. Stuff it in and take care of others. He was taught at the mere age of eight to stuff emotions and feelings in to take care of others. He learned to not show his hurt to help his siblings with theirs. Guess how he chose to do that? You got it: humor. Even as an adult, he is hilarious, but he has difficulties expressing vulnerable emotions or even listening to others. After all, laughter is the best medicine!

Vulnerable with God

Recently in a Bible study, it occurred to me that we can't just be vulnerable with others and our spouses; we have to be vulnerable with God as well. "Aaron, I am a little confused. You said that vulnerability meant the potential to be hurt. God can't hurt us." When we are vulnerable with God, it should cost us something. If God doesn't come through, you may look foolish or fall apart, so you trust him and become vulnerable with him.

I grew up in the church, hearing stories of Jesus. I asked Jesus to come into my heart when I was still in elementary school and have tried to live as a follower of King Jesus ever since. I trusted God with my heart, but that's not the last time I have to trust him. God is continually asking me to go deeper and further in my walk, and it is a vulnerable, scary, yet beautiful place to be. On July 12, 2008, I married my best friend, and I chose to honor her and love her and lay my life down for her. Can you imagine what would happen if a few days after that I told Hannah, "I'm glad that's over!" and then took my heart back to live as if I were single, without a care in the world? I married her that day, but every day I get to choose to be vulnerable or not. It's just like that with God. I made him Lord of my life in my youth, but if our relationship stopped growing there, I would question that he was ever Lord of my life in the first place.

The only way my relationship with the Lord continues to grow deeper and richer is if he gets more and more of me. Yes, I gave him all of me when I was a kid, but the older I get there is more to give. Do you really trust God with the deepest parts of your soul? There are moments in your life when God may ask you take a leap of faith in your vulnerable walk with him.

When Hannah and I were family planning, we knew that adoption was in our future. We had attempted to have biological kids for a while before realizing that God's best choice for us was adoption. We announced to our families and the world that we were called to adopt. Hannah and I made videos and told everyone that we were going to adopt. We told them in January 2013. We knew we wanted to adopt, but we weren't sure what direction to go after that. We didn't feel a clear direction toward private infant adoption or foster to adopt, so we pushed pause and waited on God. Private infant adoption would come at a large financial cost, but the foster-to-adopt program risks fostering a child who may be returned to their birth family, since that is the original goal of fostering. In that season of pain, we were not sure if fostering was for our family. We prayed for direction. We wanted a family, and we trusted God, but we were also really worried about the cost of private infant adoption. I prayed about it for weeks, maybe months, and then felt a peace. I felt God telling me to trust him and take the step toward private infant adoption.

I was still working at the bank, and I had a coworker open a savings account that I nicknamed Adoption Savings and transferred all that I had to put in the account for the moment—50 dollars. God doesn't care about the size of the gift; he cares about the heart and the cost of the gift. I told Hannah my feelings that night and showed her what I had opened up that day. In her own quiet times, the Lord was working on her heart; she also felt the Lord telling her that we were supposed to take the daunting road of private infant adoption. She had already begun nesting, searching Pinterest, and getting her boards ready.

> "God doesn't care about the size of the gift; he cares about the heart and the cost of the gift."

When both spouses are seeking the Lord on the same issue, you should land at the same place. God isn't going to send one partner one direction and another a different one. There are times when I get direction before Hannah does, and there are moments when Hannah gets direction sooner, but we have never heard God leading us in different directions. You and your spouse are one and should move as one. Wait on God to give direction. We both felt God leading in this direction, so we began to act on that belief. We trusted that God wanted us to go the route of private infant adoption, so we took a giant leap of faith and said, "God if you are calling us down this path then the answer is yes. You are going to have to do something amazing, financially, but nevertheless the answer is yes." We had already told the world we were adopting, and seven months later we were ready to move forward with whatever God had in store. As many of you know, what may seem impossible with man is not impossible for God (Luke 18:27). That Friday night, we had dinner with some friends. After dinner, as we enjoyed our chips and salsa, our friends said that they had something they wanted to tell us. They stated that a year ago they felt God telling them to save for an adoption, and that they thought they might be adopting children for themselves. However, over the previous few days, they felt God reveal to them that they were not saving for their own adoption, but for ours. They handed me a check.

"When both spouses are seeking the Lord on the same issue, you should land at the same place. God isn't going to send one partner one direction and another a different one."

I was so touched that I didn't even look at the check at first. I was already thanking them. He asked me if I had even looked at the check. It was 14,000 dollars! Every time I've told this story, I get choked up. God is so good! He took our vulnerable hearts and did something that we could have never predicted. We always knew that God could do more than we could ever think or imagine (Eph. 3:20), but even that blew our minds. God wanted us to be vulnerable and trusting to show us that he could do more than we could ever imagine. Within the next five months, we raised the rest of the money and even had extra to help finalize our adoption, because later that year, our kiddos came home. God took our 50 dollars and vulnerable faith and brought us twins and so many clothes and diapers that we didn't buy diapers for four months. We didn't buy clothes until our kids were 18 months old!

Vulnerability is the potential to be hurt. It was then and still can be scary, but we've learned that we would rather be vulnerable and waiting on the Lord than withholding our hearts and trusting in our own vices.

God or the Promise

One of the best examples from the Bible of vulnerability with God is the story of Abraham and Isaac in Genesis 22. Abraham was a guy who loved God, and God saw his love and faithfulness and called on him. God told Abraham that he was going to make a covenant with him and that his descendants would be more than the stars. We live in Houston, so at night we may see five or six stars. That doesn't seem like a large promise. But I've been out in the country before, where the night sky takes on a new perspective. Away from all the lights and busyness of the city, you can look up and see God's night-light display. There are the same number of stars in the sky whether you're in a big city or out in the country, but the city obstructs your view. If I were buying show tickets to the star display, I would get a better deal in the city because my ticket would say "obstructed view," but I would also not see the full extent of the show. I think it is safe to say that Abraham would have the ticket that said "best view around." When he looked up at the sky he was not near large city lights or obstruction. His view was completely unobstructed and serene; all that he could see was God's bright, organic skyline. I think it looked like a more upscale downtown skyline but organically created by the Creator of the Universe. I think it was glorious; stars covered the entire sky.

It is this moment that God tells Abraham that he is going to make his descendants more than the stars in the sky. He tells him that he will not even be able to count them all. That is a lot of descendants. What an amazing promise. Abraham was 75 years old when this promise came to him. Even though men and women lived a lot longer in the Bible, men and women were not having babies in their 80s or 90s.

When Abraham turned 90, he got a little tired of waiting. I don't blame him; he'd been waiting on a promise from God for 15 years and not heard anything yet. His wife came up with a secondary plan for him to sleep with her maidservant in order to carry on the bloodline. Abraham went along with the plan instead of continuing to wait on God. Abraham and his wife Sarah decided that their plan was better than God's, and we know that anytime we try our plan over God's, it doesn't usually work out so well. Abraham slept with the other woman and conceived a child. This decision was the beginning of the conflict in the Middle East as we know it. God made the covenant between Abraham and Sarah, not between Abraham and his wife's maidservant. So, even though he had a firstborn son, his firstborn son was not going to get the blessing and favor that God had intended. If God tells you to go in a specific direction, go. You'll save yourself and possibly future generations a lot in the process.

Finally, it happened. Abraham and his wife conceived a child. Abraham was 100 years old when his son Isaac was born, 25 years after the promise. Fast forward somewhere between 16 and 22 years later and God asked Abraham if he could be vulnerable with him once again by sacrificing Isaac to the Lord! You may have thought Isaac was a young boy, but that is not the case. Scholars say that he was anywhere between 16 and 22 years of age; he was old enough to carry all of the lumber for the sacrifice. But Abraham trusted God with his son, now a grown man, immediately heading to the mountain to sacrifice his son—and Isaac willingly went along. I think

Isaac knew what was happening, and he was also being vulnerable with God. I once heard a pastor say that he felt Abraham was basically saying what Jesus said in the garden of Gethsemane before he was arrested: "If this cup can pass from my hands, let it pass." If that was Abraham's prayer, then Isaac's was "Father, into your hands I commit my spirit." This was a sacrifice from the father and the son. God did not allow Abraham to hurt his son and instead provided a ram for the sacrifice. God was showing them that the ultimate sacrifice would be Christ, a spotless lamb.

I think God was testing Abraham and Isaac to see if he had their hearts. He knew that Abraham loved and followed him, but would he still continue to trust with the risk of losing the promise that finally came to pass?

Talk about being vulnerable! I can't imagine what Abraham and Isaac went through. They had trusted God, God had come through, and now God was testing them again. God tests us for our refinement and growth. He is continuing to work out our salvation with fear and trembling (Phil. 2:12). Just as I am vulnerable with my wife and have the potential for her to hurt me, we have to put our hearts on the line with God as well. We put our all into him, and if he doesn't come through, then it is all in vain. God always comes through; it just may not look the way we want it to.

I think it is interesting that when Abraham died, he had only eight sons. That doesn't sound like more than the stars to me. The Bible says that all God's promises are yes and amen (2 Cor. 1:20), which tells me in this story that just because the promise is made to us doesn't mean that the promise will be fulfilled in our lifetime. God's promise to Abraham was fulfilled, but Abraham didn't get to see the full fruition of that promise. We must be vulnerable and trust God no matter what promises we have or have not received in order to help lead future generations closer to God than they were before we were here. Make it easier for them to get to God because you were born.

Vulnerability Is Key

If you look at our rule sign in the back of the book, you will notice that this rule is not the last one on the board. I am switching it around for a purpose. I am doing that because I truly believe that vulnerability is key to having a successful relationship with God and your spouse. The last of the three things from my list from Colorado is that I had to pursue Hannah's heart above all else, besides the Lord. I had to choose to lay down my life repeatedly with the idea that she may not treat it well.

In his book *The Four Loves*, C. S. Lewis says, "To love at all is to be vulnerable. Love anything and your heart will be wrung and possibly broken. If you want to make sure of keeping it intact, you must give it to no one, not even an animal. Wrap it carefully round with hobbies and little luxuries; avoid all entanglements. Lock it up safe in the casket or coffin of your selfishness. But in that casket, safe, dark, motionless, airless, it will change. It will not be broken; it will become unbreakable, impenetrable, irredeemable. To love is to be vulnerable."[1] Love equals vulnerability. If you want to love, then you have to learn how to be vulnerable.

Hillsong is a church in Australia. They have a worship

band that has created some of the most amazing and powerful worship songs of this generation. One of their songs is called "Oceans."[2]

This song came out the year that I lost my job, 2013. There is a lyric in this song that makes me emotional every time I sing it. The bridge of this song talks about the Spirit leading you where your trust has no borders. There are times when I'm not sure if I want to trust God that blindly. I don't always want to go deeper and trust him to walk on water. That is a scary song request. Do you want to go wherever God calls you? Do you want to lose your job? Do you want to put all that you have into God? I think the only way our relationship with God moves forward is by saying yes to that question. It's scary, yes, but bold.

Just as that is the only way to continue our relationship progress with the Lord, the same is true in marriage. The only way I will continue to grow more intimate and connected to Hannah is if I continue to put my heart on the line and give her all that I have to give.

Being vulnerable brings the potential to be hurt, but it also brings the potential for blessing. When we withhold vulnerability, we may not get hurt, but we may be missing out on the potential blessing and strength that the Lord wants to provide you with. 2 Corinthians 12:10 states, *"When I am weak, then I am strong."* My vulnerability allows God to have the power and control, to really hold me close. If you're hurt by your spouse or your family, you're held closer to the Father who loves you and embraces you when you are hurting; he comforts you in the midst of the pain. Vulnerability leads to intimacy with the Father.

I chose to end the rules with this one because I

wanted the last thing you read before the closing to be the significant importance of vulnerability. It's my experience and understanding that many people do not know how to be vulnerable. What I have attempted to do in this entire book is put my heart on a platter of vulnerability, to teach you what vulnerability looks like. You have a lot of power right now. You can send me hate mail or mean emails, since my contact information is at the end of this book. You have the potential to hurt me if you choose. But, I have also decided that I can't control what you do. I am a powerful person, just like you are. I choose how to respond, act, or react, and that choice is completely mine. You have the same power. I have a mandate to be vulnerable and raw and to trust God's plan and direction. God called me to write a book, and I pray it touches people and changes hearts. I had to write this book even if only my wife and I read it. How can I expect people and couples to be vulnerable if I'm not willing to be vulnerable myself?

Now you know what vulnerability looks like, and now you have the choice to be vulnerable or not to be. If you want to continue to move forward in your walk with the Lord and your spouse, then you now know how to do it.

CHAPTER 12

After the Rules

*"Legacy. What is a legacy? It's planting seeds in
a garden you never get to see."*

—Hamilton: An American Musical

I want to leave you with a few nuggets to leave you hungry and excited as well as optimistic knowing that you can do this. We just went over several concepts; some of them may be new concepts or ideas to you, and some may not be. You can do them all, although you can't do it right all the time—so thank God for grace. You can extend grace to your spouse as well as they try to be better and more devoted to Christ and to your marriage.

One of our life phrases is *Be Intentional*. This started with my wife and her calling as a creator. She stated that she had to be intentional with her purpose or else it would get lost in the busyness that her life entails. We have since adopted this phrase and applied it to our entire life. Be intentional. If we're not intentional, things will not change. We have to plan on making a difference and then do it. If we're not intentional and purposeful with our time and behaviors, then we'll go right back to following our current synapses. Make a plan and then execute it, one synapse at a time. This is how you incorporate date nights and learning about your spouse and being honest and loving well. This is how you do it all.

If I want to have a date night with my wife, but we never set a day and time to make it happen, it won't happen. We may have good intentions, but good intentions do not get our date accomplished. We need to sit down and decide a date and time, and then we need to get babysitting taken care of if the goal of this date is a romantic night out. Dates don't always have to be romantic, but they are moments to go deeper in your connection with your spouse. Some of our dates are simply coffee at our dining table before the kids get up. We do family dates, but we also need one-on-one date time. You don't have to have all the details figured out, but you should at least figure out a day to make it happen; then you can feel free to let the wind take you where it blows. Intentionality is the only way to make something be part of the synapses.

> "Intentionality is the only way to make something be part of the synapses."

Four Options

Another nugget for you is to ask what your spouse needs when they express a stress, frustration, struggle, or difficulty. There are four options for you to choose from. (There is a fifth that other people throw out there, but I disagree and will tell you why.)

Here is the example we are going to use. I've just come home from work, and I tell Hannah that I am stressed out because I was late for work and it threw my whole day off.

The first option for her to express to me is sympathy. Sympathy has a bad rap. There are times when all your spouse wants is sympathy. There is a whole section of Hallmark cards labeled "sympathy." It's telling your spouse, "That stinks. I'm sorry that happened."

The second option is empathy. Empathy is by far the hardest of these four possible options and has two manifestations. Empathy says, "I've been there, done that, and get it." It can also say, "I haven't been there, but I want to experience and feel what you are going through right now. What does it feel like to have your whole day thrown off because you were late?" The more I do what I do for a living, the more I doubt that the first manifestation of empathy really exists. I get it that sometimes we want to know we are not alone and not the only person to ever experience what we are going through. At the same time, when I lost my grandmother, my sister and I experienced grief differently. I didn't want to tell her that I got how she felt. I wanted to put myself in her shoes to understand what it felt like for her to lose her grandmother, not what it felt like for me to lose my grandmother. The reason this option is so much harder is because it requires you to set aside your entire agenda and be really curious about what someone is going through. Don't assume you know.

The third option is to encourage. "That's okay, babe. I'm sure you still had a great day. You're going to be awesome tomorrow." That is a great response because it lets them know that even though they struggled, you are still for them and not against them. You're letting them know that their struggle or perceived failure does not change your love for them, and you are still their biggest fan.

Option four is an option we have mentioned before—fixing it. You're welcome, friends; I've given you permission to actually fix it. "Let's make sure your alarm is set correctly; that way this never happens again." Or, "Next time, don't spend as much time in the shower polishing your dome, and you'll be on time. Why do you worry so much about that thing anyway?" At times we want a fix.

All four responses are possible depending on the situation, the person, or the timing of the event. So how do you know which to respond with? Simple. Ask, "What do you need from me right now? Would you like me to show sympathy, empathy, encouragement, or help?" People may not know what they want, but if you're able to give them options, they can usually weed through them and pick the best option in that moment.

If I wanted Hannah to encourage me, but she chose fixing it, then I would feel hurt and rejected. I already felt like a failure for showing up late, and then she validated my mistake and insulted my precious dome. Most people have a default response that they want, but that default may not be the same as their spouse's. My default is encouragement and possibly help, unless we're in an argument. Then I want her to empathize and sympathize with me. It's complicated, and we often change what we want, so feel free to ask your spouse. And please try not to be offended when they ask; they're showing that they care, not that they don't get you.

Here's the fifth option: just listen. I can't stand this option, and I don't really think anybody wants it when they're expressing something that is anything deeper than surface level. Can you imagine if Hannah described her horrible day and why she felt that she was a bad mom, and all that I did was look at her? I engage her eyes, full eye contact as she has requested, and nod my head at appropriate points; but when she's done, I have nothing to say at all. I think she would feel that I was not listening at all. How could she express all of that while I just stare deadpan at her? That is ridiculous. Of course, active listening is important, and I don't want to be too quick to respond, but at some point she is going to want something from me. She wants a response or a gesture, such as a hug from me, which is where the other options come in. She also does not want me to change the subject and then ask her, "So, what's for dinner?" Talk about seeing the wrath of a redhead. The only time that I think I want Hannah to *just* listen is when the topic is of no real concern. "Babe, how 'bout them Cowboys or Texans!" (I know it may be weird that I pull for both. A client once told me that was the therapist in me, just pulling for everyone to win. Maybe so.) When I express this to her, I don't really need her full attention or some brilliant moment of truth. I'm just telling her because she is my wife, and I want to tell her everything. (Pray for her, because there are a lot of things that I want her to just listen to.)

All by Myself

I could not end this book without talking to the person who has read this book and feels all alone. I commend you. This is not an easy journey, and it can feel even harder when you feel that you're doing it alone. I want to encourage you to start praying for your spouse. Pray that they find their identity in God and his calling. Even if you have a difficult time seeing it in them, try to start pulling out the *imago Dei* that we discussed. Continue to ask God to help you do your part and to trust him with the rest. If you are in an abusive relationship, please take safety precautions. God is not asking you to stay and continue to be beaten or abused. Please reach out to your faith community to get some help; nobody wants the abusive relationship to continue on the path that it is headed. Reach out to the elders in your church for assistance. We want to get you and your spouse the help needed. Get in a good community of believers to do life with. I do not mean somewhere you can go to bash your spouse, but a community that will love you where you are, broken and hurt. We are all broken, so don't feel that you have to pretend that you are okay. It is okay to not be okay.

"Start praying for your spouse."

I am praying for you more than you know. I am praying for your spouse and for your entire family. I want you to know that God can change this around. Proverbs 21:1 states, *"A king's heart is like streams of water in the Lord's hand: He directs it wherever He chooses."* God can breathe into any situation, and it will change the course in an instant. Keep persevering. James 1:2 states to consider it all joy when you're going through trials.

I am not in the career of divorce counseling. I am a therapist who fights for marriages. If God could not save marriages and redeem them and make them look like Christ, I would not do what I do for a living. There is always hope in God. Don't trust the power of your own self or your own will; only with God can your marriage be a testimony worth sharing! He has the power to do the impossible; even when all hope feels lost, he has not forgotten you. He loves you and cares for you and wants your relationship to look like him. Continue to be the bride of Christ and know that he is a great groom. Don't give up. It may seem difficult or daunting, and it may be, but you never know when your day four is coming. (Remember, Lazarus was raised from the dead on day four.) You may be in the middle of waiting. Know that God still cares. He hears your heart and catches your tears. In fact, he is crying harder than you because it breaks his heart more than yours that your marriage is not where it is supposed to be . . . yet.

Audience of One

The more I've studied marriages, including my own, the more I have realized that marriage is actually very simple. All I have to do in marriage is worry about me. I cannot control my spouse or my kids. All I can do is be responsible and accountable for myself. This is a freeing realization because I no longer have to be responsible for my kids' or my wife's freedom. Jesus has called us all to be free, but the only person I can control is me. I need to work on me. I know difficult times will come. I have always said that marriages need to have insurance. Insurance is what you have on your car, your home, and maybe even your life. The thing about insurance is that you have to have it before you need it. Flood insurance does no good if you call after the flood has occurred. I can't call the flood insurance company after the flood and ask them to help me with my water damage. "Yes, I was calling to ask for coverage on the flood that just occurred and damaged my home. No, I do not have current coverage; I didn't know I needed it until the storm came. So if you can please help me with that, I would greatly appreciate it. Thanks." Did you catch it? Didn't think I needed it. You need it. I think marriage is just like this. People are sometimes confused and caught off guard the moment trouble or strife comes into the marriage.

> "When you are vulnerable with God and your spouse, you are engaging in spiritual warfare."

I have stated this to couples in counseling and firmly believe it: if you are not experiencing some sort of strife or difficult time in your life or in your marriage, then I'm not sure that the devil thinks you are much of a threat. The devil comes to steal, kill, and destroy (John 10:10); if he is leaving you alone, then he just may think there is nothing there to destroy. When you experience a trial in your marriage, parenting, finances, or health, then know that the devil is fighting hard to keep you from your destiny. When difficulties or troubles come, choose to push toward Christ and pray that your home will be stronger as a result of the refining process. God always wins! Even in the midst of the storm, God is still on the throne!

Hannah and I have struggles and arguments. Believe it or not, we have even had arguments in the process of writing this book. I am writing a book on living a marriage more Christlike, yet I have had arguments with my wife while writing it.

Since I started writing the book, I have been diagnosed with arthritis at the ripe age of 32, a disease which has made it painful to type. I wore a splint since the beginning of this book, and my wife has experienced difficult medical problems that resulted in having brain surgery. My father-in-law has been in and out of the hospital in a battle with cancer. Times are not always rosy. Know that if you decide you want your marriage to look more like Jesus, then it's going to anger the devil. He wants you to stay complacent in your marriage and maybe even kill your marriage. When you are vulnerable with God and your spouse, you are engaging in spiritual warfare. Your fight is not against flesh and blood but principalities of the dark (Eph. 6:12). It is a war, but a war worth fighting. Go ahead and purchase the insurance, and know that when war comes, you will be ready. You already know that the attacks and struggles will not end you and will not destroy your home. In fact, they are going to make you stronger and more trusting in the Lord than ever before. The finished product doesn't always look the way you intended it to. I didn't want to get fired. I didn't want to go through infertility. I didn't want my father-in-law to become ill. What I want more than anything is for God to tell me, "Well done good and faithful servant" (Matt. 25:23 NIV). We serve an audience of one.

Acknowledgments

Thanks to:

As One. You all are amazing and life-giving. Thanks for being my community and family.

Jerrell and Kay Altic, who encouraged me to write this book and continued to love and support me throughout the process.

John and Cynthia Gualy. You love people where they are. All feel welcome and loved in your presence, but you encourage them to continue to grow in order to reach their full potential in Christ. Thanks so much for doing that for all of those around you, including me and my family. You are a true example of service and using your talents and gifts for the Lord.

Omar and Joanna Calderon. You are both special people to know. The love and vulnerability that you express is refreshing and special. Thanks for your love and fervent prayers. I am honored to call you friends.

Adam Mason. Thanks for believing in me and helping me get my counseling career started. You invested in my potential as a counselor and I am forever grateful for your love and support in helping launch my career.

Sean Ringrose. There are no words that express how great of a friend you have been to me. You are my longest friend and I am forever grateful for your love and support and for always listening to me. You were one of the first people who let me share openly and honestly. Thanks for being consistent and a loving brother.

Scott and Sarah Anthony. You guys are truly a blessing. Your love and compassion is so special. You guys are incredible, and we are honored to know you guys and call you family. Our kids love spending time with Ms. Sarah and Mr. Scott!

Angie Brigle. Thanks for investing in me and the work I am doing and just leading with a "yes." I love your spirit and eagerness in helping me launch this book.

Nathan and Kristen Stedham. You guys are a true example of quiet leadership. Your love and resolve to lead and love well without making a show is something special to watch. You guys are amazing and I love that I get to watch you guys love with such grace and elegance.

Kenny and Candice Corley. You guys are rockstars. Thanks for continuing to love our family well. We are honored to call you friends and so excited that God brought you into our lives. Thanks for always encouraging me and my family. We can always count on you no matter what you have going on. You love well at all times!

Josh and Heather Pritchard. Thanks for believing in me and my vision for marriages. I was so excited when you and your family first walked into the bank so many years ago. I am thankful that our friendship has continued long past the banking world as we continue to love others well by being brothers and sisters in Christ.

Hannah, my love. You are incredible and I love doing life with you. I am so honored that God brought us together and my greatest passion in life is loving Jesus with you. You are such a beauty and a grace-filled woman that I thank God everyday for, giving me a woman who strives to look like Jesus on the regular. Thanks for loving me well and encouraging me all the way through. You have been my greatest cheerleader and your love and sacrifice you make for our family does not go unnoticed.

Jesus Christ, my Savior and the reason I live. I am so grateful and humbled to be an ambassador for your love and direction. Thank you for loving me where I am and never giving up on me. You have saved my life and given purpose to these dry bones.

Additional Resources

Brown, Brene. *I Thought It Was Just Me (but it isn't): Making the Journey from "What Will People Think?" to "I am Enough."* MP3. Brilliance Audio, 2014.

Caine, Christine. *Unashamed: Drop the Baggage, Pick up Your Freedom, Fulfill Your Destiny.* MP3. Brilliance Audio, 2016.

Cloud, Henry, and John Townsend. *Boundaries: When to Say Yes, When to Say No to Take Control of Your Life.* Zondervan Audiobook, 2015.

Laney, Marti Olsen. *The Introvert Advantage: How Quiet People Can Thrive in an Extrovert World.* Workman Publishing, 2002.

Miller, Donald. *Scary Close: Dropping the Act and Finding True Intimacy.* Thomas Nelson, 2015.

Neel, Deborah, and Douglas E. Rosenau. *Total Intimacy: A Guide to Loving by Color.* Suwanee, GA: Sexual Wholeness Resources, 2014.

Silk, Danny. *Keep Your Love On: Connection, Communication and Boundaries.* Loving on Purpose, 2015.

Works Cited

Anderson, Jared. "Amazed." *Where to Begin*. Integrity Music, 2006.

Bethel Music. "Ever Be." *We Will Not Be Shaken*. Bethel Music, 2015.

Chapman, Gary. *The Five Love Languages: How to Express Heartfelt Commitment to Your Mate*. Chicago, IL: Moody Publishers, 2004.

Crabb, Larry. *Soul Talk: The Language God Longs for Us to Speak*. Franklin, TN: Integrity Publishers, 2005.

DC Talk. "Luv is a Verb." *Free at Last*. Mark Heimermann and TobyMac, 1992.

Dictionary.com. "Conflict." Online edition. 2016. http://www.dictionary.com/browse/conflict?s=t

Gottman, John M., and Nan Silver. *The Seven Principles for Making Marriage Work: A Practical Guide from the Country's Foremost Relationship Expert*. New York: Three Rivers Press, 2000.

Graham, Ruth. *Billy Graham in Quotes*. Edited by Franklin Graham with Donna Lee Toney. Nashville, TN: Thomas

Nelson, 2011. http://www.dailymail.co.uk/news/article-2082385/We-1--You-need-34k-income-global-elite--half-worlds-richest-live-U-S.html

Gye, Hugo. 2012. "America IS the 1%: You need just $34,000 annual income to be in the global elite...and HALF the world's richest people live in the U.S." *The Daily Mail.* January 5.

Hillsong United. "Oceans." *Zion.* Hillsong, 2013.

Indiana Jones and the Last Crusade. Directed by Steven Spielberg. CA: Paramount Pictures, 1989.

King, Martin Luther, Jr. *Strength to Love.* New York: Harper & Row, 1963.

Lewis, C. S. *The Chronicles of Narnia: The Lion, the Witch and the Wardrobe.* New York: Scholastic, 1987.

Lewis, C. S. *The Four Loves.* London: Geoffrey Bles, 1960.

The Princess Bride. Directed by Rob Reiner. CA: Act III Communications, 1987.

Thomas, Gary. *Sacred Marriage: What if God Designed Marriage to Make Us Holy More Than to Make Us Happy.* Grand Rapids: Zondervan, 2002.

US Department of Health and Human Services. "Eating Disorder Statistics." *National Association of Anorexia Nervosa and Associated Disorders,* 2017. http://www.anad.org/get-information/about-eating-disorders/eating-disorders-statistics/

Warren, Rick. *The Purpose Driven Life: What on Earth Am I Here For*. Grand Rapids: Zondervan, 2002.

YouTube. "Endorphin Casually Walks to Music." Posted by Paul Messing, December 11, 2015. https://www.youtube.com/watch?v=n7UFDUcstW0

Endnotes

Chapter 1

1. Sorry, I couldn't resist starting a book on marriage with a fantastic quote from one of my favorite movies of all time.

2. A League of Their Own, directed by Penny Marshall (Culver City, CA: Columbia Tristar Home Video, 2004).

Chapter 2

1. Bethel Music, "Ever Be," *We Will Not Be Shaken* (Bethel Music, 2015).

2. *Indiana Jones and the Last Crusade*, directed by Steven Spielberg (CA: Paramount Pictures, 1989).

3. Gary Thomas, *Sacred Marriage: What If God Designed Marriage to Make Us Holy More Than to Make Us Happy?* (Grand Rapids: Zondervan, 2002).

4. C. S. Lewis, *The Chronicles of Narnia: The Lion, the Witch and the Wardrobe (New York: Scholastic, 1987), 79–80.*

Chapter 7

1. Hugo Guy, "America IS the 1%: You need just $34,000 annual income to be in the global elite...and HALF the world's richest people live in the U.S.," *The Daily Mail,* January 5, 2012.

2. Jared Anderson, "Amazed," *Where to Begin* (Integrity Music, 2006).

3. Ruth Graham, *Billy Graham in Quotes, eds. Franklin Graham with Donna Lee Toney (Nashville: Thomas Nelson, 2011).*

4. Gary Chapman, *The Five Love Languages: How to Express Heartfelt Commitment to Your Mate* (Chicago, IL: Moody Publishers, 2004).

5. DC Talk, "Luv is a Verb," *Free at Last (Mark Heimermann and TobyMac, 1992).*

Chapter 8

1. John M. Gottman and Nan Silver, *The Seven Principles for Making Marriage Work: A Practical Guide from the Country's Foremost Relationship Expert (New York: Three Rivers Press, 2000), 130.*

2. Dictionary.com, s.v. "Conflict," accessed October 29, 2016, www.dictionary.com/browse/conflict?s=t.

Chapter 9

1. John M. Gottman and Nan Silver, *The Seven Principles for Making Marriage Work: A Practical Guide from the Country's Foremost Relationship Expert (New York: Three Rivers Press, 2000), 281.*

2. "Endorphin Casually Walks to Music," YouTube video, posted by Paul Messing, December 11, 2015, https://www.youtube.com/watch?v=n7UFDUcstW0.

Chapter 10

1. Rick Warren, *The Purpose Driven Life: What on Earth Am I Here For (Grand Rapids: Zondervan, 2002)*.

2. U.S. Department of Health and Human Services, "Eating Disorder Statistics," accessed October 10, 2017, http://www.anad.org/get-information/about-eating-disorders/eating-disorders-statistics/.

3. Larry Crabb, *Soul Talk: The Language God Longs for Us to Speak* (Franklin, TN: Integrity Publishers, 2005).

Chapter 11

1. C. S. Lewis, *The Four Loves (London: Geoffrey Bles, 1960)*.

2. Hillsong United, "Oceans," *Zion* (Hillsong, 2013).

Get in touch with Aaron at:

www.astrongerknot.com
astrongerknot@gmail.com